# JEFF CORWIN

# ANIMALS
# AND HABITATS
# OF THE
# UNITED STATES

**PUFFIN BOOKS**
An Imprint of Penguin Group (USA) Inc.

To Maya, Marina, and Natasha

PUFFIN BOOKS
Published by the Penguin Group
Penguin Young Readers Group, 345 Hudson Street, New York, New York 10014, U.S.A.
Penguin Group (Canada), 90 Eglinton Avenue East, Suite 700,
Toronto, Ontario, Canada M4P 2Y3 (a division of Pearson Penguin Canada Inc.)
Penguin Books Ltd, 80 Strand, London WC2R 0RL, England
Penguin Ireland, 25 St Stephen's Green, Dublin 2, Ireland (a division of Penguin Books Ltd)
Penguin Group (Australia), 250 Camberwell Road, Camberwell, Victoria 3124, Australia
(a division of Pearson Australia Group Pty Ltd)
Penguin Books India Pvt Ltd, 11 Community Centre, Panchsheel Park, New Delhi - 110 017, India
Penguin Group (NZ), 67 Apollo Drive, Rosedale, North Shore 0632, New Zealand
(a division of Pearson New Zealand Ltd.)
Penguin Books (South Africa) (Pty) Ltd, 24 Sturdee Avenue,
Rosebank, Johannesburg 2196, South Africa

Registered Offices: Penguin Books Ltd, 80 Strand, London WC2R 0RL, England

Published by Puffin Books, a division of Penguin Young Readers Group, 2009

1 3 5 7 9 10 8 6 4 2

LIBRARY OF CONGRESS CATALOGING-IN-PUBLICATION DATA IS AVAILABLE.

Puffin Books ISBN 978-0-14-241405-7

Printed in the United States of America

FSC
Mixed Sources
Product group from well-managed
forests, controlled sources and
recycled wood or fiber
Cert no. SCS-COC-00648
www.fsc.org
© 1996 Forest Stewardship Council

# CONTENTS

# INTRODUCTION
## WHAT IS AN ECOSYSTEM?

**W**elcome to the fascinating world of ecosystems! In this book we'll take a look at four of my favorite ecosystems on Earth. They're as different as night from day, or as a desert from an underwater forest. But in each one, you'll see how living and nonliving things connect as they all struggle to survive.

*Eco* comes from an old Greek word that means "house" or "household." *System*—well, you know what system means. Something with many parts. Something in which all the parts work together.

A house where all the parts work together?

Sure. A house or a home is a place where someone, or something, lives. Think of your home—and all that it has inside it—shelter from the cold and wind and rain, food to eat, a family to take care of you. Your home holds the stuff you need so that you can keep on living. Whether you live in a three-story house or an apartment or an igloo, your house has a system—a lot of interconnected parts—so that living things (you and your family) can survive there.

So what happens if you change one part of your house? That's right—the change affects everything. Suppose you leave a window open in the kitchen on a chilly day. Your mom, sitting in the dining room, is going to get cold. Or suppose you knock a hole in the floor of your bedroom. Now the living room has a hole in the ceiling. Anything that happens to one part of the house—one part of the system—changes all the other parts as well. That's what being a system means.

The natural world has many ecosystems, where living things find homes filled with whatever they need to survive. Within an ecosystem, plants and animals form relationships with each

Opposite top: A ladybug on orange-tree leaves.
Opposite middle: Jeff Corwin.
Opposite bottom: A colorful lubber grasshopper clings to grass.
Right: A great white egret with a frog in its beak.

other. A small fish eats seaweed; a bigger fish eats the smaller fish. And they form relationships with the nonliving things around them, too, like the sunlight that gives the seaweed energy to grow. All these relationships together make up an ecosystem.

You can find ecosystems wherever you go. That oak tree in your front yard? It's an ecosystem. Sunlight shines on the tree's leaves. The tree converts that sunlight into energy. Part of that energy gets stored in the form of acorns. Squirrels come along and eat those acorns. Beetles burrow beneath the tree's bark. Birds make those beetles a tasty snack. They build their nests in the tree to keep their eggs and hatchlings safe from predators. But a raccoon climbs the tree and makes a meal out of one of those precious eggs. And so on. You'd be amazed at the amount of life that can find a home in a simple ecosystem like a tree.

A tide pool in the ocean is an ecosystem, too, even one no bigger than a puddle. Sun shines on the pool, and the seaweed soaks up its energy, changing it into food in a process called **photosynthesis**. Snails graze on the seaweed. As they eat, the energy that the seaweed captured from the sun passes into the snail. A wave slops into the pool, bringing fresh nutrients—delicious plankton and bits of rotting seaweed.

Washington
Montana
North Dakota
Minnesota
Maine
Oregon
South Dakota
Wisconsin
Michigan
New York
Yellowstone
Wyoming
Nevada
Nebraska
Iowa
Illinois
Ohio
Pennsylvania
Utah
Colorado
Indiana
Monterey Bay
California
Kansas
Missouri
Kentucky
Virginia
Oklahoma
Arkansas
Tennessee
North Carolina
Arizona
New Mexico
South Carolina
Sonoran Desert
Texas
Mississippi
Alabama
Georgia
Louisiana
Florida
Everglades

Opposite top: A striped bass.
Opposite bottom: A raccoon.
Below: A crab.

Barnacles sweep this food in with their feathery legs. A crab darts out from a sheltering rock. A sea star stalks a mussel clinging to the same rock. This tiny puddle on the edge of the sea is full of living things doing what living things do— mostly trying to eat and not get eaten. If they succeed at both, they'll survive.

But ecosystems don't have to be small. Consider a pond. Or an ocean. Or a forest. Or a mountain. Each of these is an eco- system, providing living things with what they need for survival.

# YELLOWSTONE

Imagine a place where mud boils and stinks like rotten eggs. Where wolf packs howl and bald eagles swoop down to catch cutthroat trout. Where steam bursts from the ground and trees have turned to stone.

That's Yellowstone National Park. The park covers about 2.2 million acres, mostly in Wyoming, overlapping a little into Idaho and Montana. It was the first national park in the world, created in 1872 by President

Right: A bull elk walking along a river in Yellowstone National Park.

Ulysses S. Grant to be "a public park or pleasuring ground for the benefit and enjoyment of the people." Nestled in the eastern edge of the Rocky Mountains, Yellowstone has peaks and plains, forests of lodgepole pine trees and meadows of wildflowers, rivers and lakes, and some of the coolest animals around—elk, wolves, bison, bears, bald eagles, and mountain lions, to name a few.

And as most people know, Yellowstone also has geysers. In fact, Yellowstone has two-thirds of the geysers on the entire planet—more than the rest of the world put together! It has boiling mud pots and steaming hot springs, too. All of Yellowstone's **geothermic** wonders happen because it's a place where the crust of rock and dirt that makes up the surface of the planet is thin—in places it's only about three miles deep. Underneath that crust is a layer of hot liquid rock called **magma**.

That thin crust of earth and the boiling magma not far underneath mean that Yellowstone is actually a giant volcano, so big it's called a super volcano. It's one of the most geologically active places on the planet—which means that cool stuff happens when that magma under the ground finds ways to the surface.

In the past, the volcano that is Yellowstone erupted more than once. Lava (which is what magma

A portion of a petrified tree trunk.

is called once it's no longer underground) and hot ash spewed into the air to rain down on nearby trees, sometimes burying forests fifteen feet deep. These trees then died, but they didn't fall over. The ash held them upright. Slowly the trees rotted away, and minerals in the ash took their place.

A geyser in Yellowstone Lake.

Mammoth Hot Springs in Yellowstone National Park.

The trees became petrified, meaning they turned to stone.

And then a new forest grew on top of the old one—and it happened again. And again.

The most recent huge eruption happened 630,000 years ago. A massive volcano in the center of what's now the park erupted in an explosion a thousand times more powerful than Mount St. Helens in 1980. The volcano's peak collapsed, creating a crater, or **caldera**, that became the Central Plateau and that is now the location of Yellowstone Lake. From several spots inside the park, you can see the curving line of mountains that mark the edge of this ancient caldera.

In one place in Yellowstone, twenty-seven forests grew in layers, one on top of the other, each one buried in ash as volcanoes erupted time and time again.

FASCINATING FACT

Lava flowed and cooled, creating rock formations that cracked and shifted from the heat of the magma still trapped below the earth.

One day, volcanoes could erupt in Yellowstone once more. But the lake of magma under the thin crust of earth is better known for making **geysers**—bursts of hot water and steam that explode from holes in the ground.

This is how a geyser happens.

Rain falls and soaks into the ground. It trickles and drips down until it reaches a layer of rock just above the pool of magma. Here's the thing about magma—it's hot. So rocks right above it are hot, too, hot enough to turn some of that water into steam and send it rising back up toward the surface. Then a couple of things can happen.

If the water gets blocked, it builds up more and more pressure until it can burst loose in a plume of water and steam called a geyser. You've probably heard of the most popular geyser in Yellowstone—Old Faithful. It goes off "faithfully" approximately

Above: Old Faithful geyser erupting at sunset.
Below: A geyser in Yellowstone Lake.
Opposite: Yellowstone's Beehive geyser erupting.

11

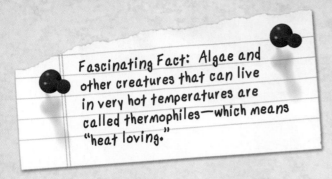

every seventy minutes. It needs that time to build up enough pressure for the hot water and steam to be forced up to the surface.

In other places around Yellowstone, water that's heated by the magma underground doesn't get blocked on its way to the surface. Then it bubbles out of the ground in a hot spring. If that spring doesn't get enough water, it becomes a mud pot—a puddle of boiling goop. Some of the hot springs in Yellowstone smell of sulfur—a stench like rotten eggs—because of minerals and bacteria that the water picks up while deep underground.

You wouldn't think that anything as hot, and smelly, and just plain weird as a hot spring could be an ecosystem. But living things can survive in the strangest of places. You won't find fish or frogs or water lilies in Yellowstone's hot springs. But algae thrives. In fact, you can tell the temperature of a hot spring just by looking at its algae. If the pool is green, it's at a temperature of 120 degrees Fahrenheit or less—it's full of an algae that

doesn't grow if the water gets any hotter. Orange algae means the water is about 145 degrees, yellow means it might be up to 160 degrees, and a clear blue pool means it's too hot for algae to grow there at all.

The geysers and hot springs and petrified forests were what first got people interested in protecting Yellowstone as a national park. But there is a lot more to this ecosystem than boiling mud pots and colorful algae. Yellowstone was also home to some fascinating animals. And soon people realized that these animals needed protection, too.

Here's the thing—those animals didn't live in a park. (They still don't.) They live in an ecosystem, and that ecosystem stretches far beyond the boundaries of Yellowstone National Park. It's called the Greater Yellowstone Ecosystem, and it stretches far

**Right:** Water falling on sulfur steps of Mammoth Hot Springs in Yellowstone National Park.

**Top, far right:** A geyser in Yellowstone National Park in the Old Faithful area.

**Middle, far right:** A geothermal area in Yellowstone National Park boils and bubbles, occasionally spitting out water and steam.

**Bottom, far right:** A stream of hot water colored by bacteria and algae formations.

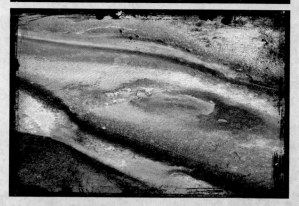

into Wyoming, Montana, and Idaho. Some people say it's 12 million acres; some say 20 million. Since 1872, more and more of this land has been brought under protection.

Today, in the Greater Yellowstone Ecosystem, there are six national forests, two national parks (including Yellowstone), three national wildlife refuges, one Native American reservation, land that belongs to the Bureau of Land Management, land that belongs to states, and land that belongs to ordinary people. If you think of the Greater Yellowstone Ecosystem as 12 million acres, then about half of that land is protected from hunting, grazing, logging, mining, roads, and building. It's a safe place for the plants and animals that depend on the wild lands of Yellowstone for their survival—from a tiny yellow glacier lily to a towering lodgepole pine tree, and from a yellow-bellied marmot to a bull moose. It also provides a home for one of North America's largest predators—the grizzly bear.

Imagine a mother grizzly, about seven feet tall if she stands up on her hind legs, as she sometimes does to check out her surroundings. This huge bear, covered in her thick brown fur (the other name for a grizzly is a brown bear), is leading her two cubs through a cool, shadowy pine forest. Not far away, sunlight falls in long shafts between the trunks of the trees, showing where a meadow can be found.

The cubs, one male and one female, were born several months ago, in the middle of winter, while their mother hibernated in her den. She didn't even wake up to greet her

Opposite: A brown bear, also known as a grizzly bear.
Above: A family of brown bears.

babies, but they drank her rich milk while she was still sleeping. They grew and grew in the dark, warm safety of the den; outside snow fell and wind blew. Now it's early summer, and they've been out in the world for a few months. Like their mother, they're eager to eat whatever they can find.

It takes a lot of food to keep a grizzly bear going. A big male bear, like the cubs' father, can weigh up to six or seven hundred pounds. This mother is smaller than that, weighing about three hundred pounds. Like other grizzlies, she'll eat just about anything—roots, berries, grass, dandelions,

Bears do not drink, eat, urinate, or defecate during hibernation. Can you imagine not going to the bathroom for months?

**FASCINATING FACT**

15

clover, thistle, nuts from pinecones (sometimes she digs up stashes hidden underground by squirrels), ants, and other insects. Despite its reputation as a fearsome hunter, a grizzly actually gets most of its nutrition from plants. But the bears do like meat when they can get it.

Cautiously, the mother grizzly pokes her head out into the clearing, her nose and

A grizzly bear's front paw print normally measures 6" to 8" (excluding the heel), and the back is approximately 10" to 12" in length.

back     front

Above: An elk doe and her spotted fawn in Yellowstone National Park.
Opposite, top: An elk doe in a grass field in Yellowstone National Park.
Opposite, bottom: A brown bear.

eyes shielded by blossoming purple fireweed. A herd of elk is grazing in the sunlight, tearing hungrily at the fresh green grass. The herd has several calves that were born in the spring, and the mother grizzly hopes to bring down one of them for a meal. Bears in Yellowstone are the number one predators of elk calves.

The cubs stay nearby so that the mother can see them as she slowly creeps out into the clearing. There are lots of threats to young grizzlies in the mountains and plains around Yellowstone, and the cubs' only protection is their mother. She's upwind of the elk, which means the breeze is blowing their scent to her, not hers to them. And a gangly elk calf, whose legs seem too long for its body, has wandered away from its mother, sniffing eagerly at the grass, nosing at wildflowers, curious to learn more about the world all around it.

It's a difficult decision for the mother bear. Should she leave her cubs and go after this tempting prey? Her cubs might be in danger if she's not there to protect them—but the elk calf could provide enough food to make a good meal.

The elk calf takes a few more steps away from its mother, still not noticing the hungry

her young, stare at each other for a few seconds. Then the bear retreats into the woods. She's been away from her cubs long enough.

But the mother and cubs are hungry. They did not find much food this morning, and they rested during the heat of the day. Now it's close to evening and they definitely need

bear. The grizzly can't resist. She gets ready to charge. For a short distance, a grizzly can run about thirty-five to forty miles per hour—faster than a car driving down the street outside of your house. Not many things can outrun a grizzly charge—and fewer still can stand up to it.

But the elk calf is lucky. Its mother looks up just in time and leaps to her calf's defense. Dashing to put herself between the calf and the grizzly, she snorts a challenge.

While the calf looks like a tasty and nutritious meal for the grizzly, her mother is something else. A full-grown elk is about the size of a horse, and its hooves are hard and sharp. One kick could injure the mother bear severely, possibly even kill her. She doesn't want to risk it. The two mothers, each one desperate to protect a meal. The cubs follow their mother uphill to a rocky slope. Along the way, one cub stops to sniff with interest at a hole beneath an overhanging rock. She doesn't know that the footprints around the hole, showing hind feet with five claws and front feet with four, mean that the animal who lives there is something better left alone—a North American porcupine.

The second biggest **rodent** in North America (only a beaver is bigger), the porcupine sleeps in its den during the day and comes out at night to feed. But the bear cub, poking its nose into the den, has woken up the porcupine. A soft chattering noise comes from inside. It's a warning. If the bear cub doesn't back off, she's likely to get something she doesn't expect—a smack in the face from a porcupine tail and a nose full of quills.

A porcupine has about thiry thousand quills. It can't shoot them, as some people think. But when it whacks an enemy with its tail, the quills come loose and stick in the other animal's flesh. A North American porcupine's quills are barbed, which means that they slide in easily but come out only if they're yanked. It's not only painful—animals can die when wounds from porcupine quills get infected.

Fortunately for the bear cub, she notices that her mother has

moved farther up the slope and she runs away from the porcupine's den before she learns a painful lesson. The cub catches up with her mother just as the big bear hooks her long, straight claws under a rock and uses her powerful shoulder muscles to flip it over. Clustered under the rock is one of the bear's favorite and most important foods—the army cutworm moth. Elk meat would have been nice, but as far as the bears are concerned, moths are easier and a lot less dangerous to catch. And they're a high-protein treat, just like the elk calf would have been.

These moths stay cool under the rocks by day, coming out to feed on flower nectar at night. A single bear can gobble up between ten thousand and forty thousand

Above: A family of brown bears fishing in a river.
Opposite: A porcupine.

moths in one day! The mother flips over several more rocks. But there aren't too many moths here today. The grizzly and her cubs are going to have to work harder if they want to find enough to eat.

Luckily, it is summer in Yellowstone, which means that more food is not too far away. Following closely behind their mother, the cubs keep pace as she leads them toward a river. There, in the shallows, is a feast that bears must dream of during their long winter sleep—cutthroat trout, returning to the place where they were born to **spawn**, or lay their eggs. Some of the trout won't survive. Lots of predators, not all of them bears, count on streams full of leaping, struggling,

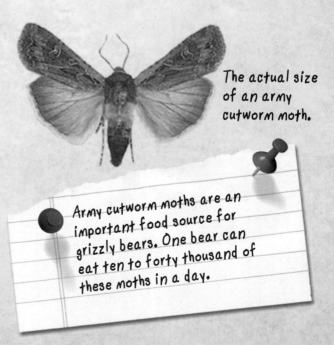

The actual size of an army cutworm moth.

Army cutworm moths are an important food source for grizzly bears. One bear can eat ten to forty thousand of these moths in a day.

Above: A river otter on a tree trunk.
Opposite: A bear fishing in Yellowstone National Park.

flashing trout to fill their stomachs and give them the energy they need to survive.

Most humans who like to fish have favorite spots, or favorite lures, or strategies that they think work best. Bears are sort of like this, too. Some stand on rocks and watch for fish to swim by. Some wade right into the current. Some even stick their heads underwater. The mother splashes into the river and chooses a spot carefully. She stands facing downstream, with the current swirling around her paws. Across the river, another hunter is also searching for fish. A river otter darts down the bank and slips into the rapids. This graceful member of the weasel family is such a quick swimmer that it can actually catch fish underwater.

The mother bear can't swim as fast as

cutthroat trout

the otter, so she finds a good place to wait. After she's stood patiently, not moving, for several minutes, a trout, fighting to get upstream, flings its silvery body out of the water. It's trying to jump some rapids—but, in fact, it jumps right at the bear. With a quick jerk of her head, the bear snatches the trout out of the air.

Clasping the thrashing fish firmly in her teeth, she carries it toward the bank. Her cubs are eagerly awaiting a taste. First their mother shakes the water from her long brown coat, giving her children a shower they weren't expecting. Then she settles down to eat the fish herself. This may seem selfish, but the mother's first job is to make sure that she stays strong and healthy enough to catch more food for her cubs and protect them from any dangers. The energy that this fish will provide is going to help her do that.

But the hungry cubs don't want to wait. One pounces on the fish's tail, despite a warning growl from his mother. He gets his teeth into the tail and rips it loose. His mother is too busy finishing the rest of the fish to object, and when his sister tries to snatch a bite for herself, the cub pushes her away. He trots a few paces along the riverbank and drops his scrap of trout on the rocks, preparing to enjoy it in peace.

But he's not going to get what he hopes

Bear cubs weigh less than a pound when they are born. (Most human babies weigh about eight pounds.) Mother bears usually have one or two cubs at a time.

**FASCINATING FACT**

for. Another hunter has been drawn to the river and to all the fish in it—only this predator doesn't hunt from the ground.

The cub is startled by a flurry of wings, a harsh screech, and a sharp, strong beak

An adult male bald eagle.

The eagle's wings, stretched out to let it glide gracefully along the air, can be longer than seventy-two inches. The setting sun flashes brightly off the white feathers of its head and tail. Only adult male bald eagles have heads covered with white feathers; females and young birds are mostly brown.

With its white head, large, curved bill, and strong talons, the bald eagle is a familiar symbol of the United States of America. But not too long ago, it looked like these eagles might not survive here. First hunting and trapping, and then pollution, made the number of bald eagles in the lower forty-eight states drop to between two and three thousand. But people rallied around the national bird. Laws were passed to forbid hunting and trapping of the birds, and then to ban some of the pesticides and other forms of pollution that were harming them. Today there are about twenty thousand bald eagles in the lower forty-eight states.

This eagle soars over a mountain slope and its shadow falls across the herd of bighorn sheep grazing there. It is a herd

less than inch from his tender nose. He jumps back as the bald eagle seizes the scrap of fish in its sharp talons and swoops back up into the air. The whole thing took only a second or two, and the cub is looking around in wonder, as if trying to figure out where his fish has gone.

The bald eagle flies to the top of a dead pine tree nearby, where it can enjoy its stolen meal. Fish is its favorite food, and although it's a skillful hunter who can swoop down and snatch fish out of the water, it's not too proud to become a thief if that's what it takes to get something to eat. Below the eagle, the mother grizzly wades back into the water to catch another fish. Her cubs may be able to snatch a bite or two of this one. The eagle, meanwhile, launches itself off the tree and takes to the skies.

A male bighorn sheep can have horns that weigh as much as thirty or forty pounds, more than the rest of the bones in his body put together.

**FASCINATING FACT**

of rams, or males; the big, curving horns on their heads make it easy to tell. In the fall, when the rams battle for mates, they run at each other, sometimes getting up to speeds of twenty miles an hour, and smash their horns together with a crack that can be heard across the mountains. Sometimes the males will fight for hours, but their thick, bony skulls usually keep them from getting hurt.

But since it isn't mating season at the moment, the herd of rams is grazing peacefully together. High up on the rocky slopes of the mountains, they are mostly safe from predators. Nimble, quick climbers, the sheep can dash up rocky slopes where it would be hard for a hunter to follow them. Even so, mountain lions sometimes stalk bighorn sheep. There are about twenty of the big cats in Yellowstone, and they are skillful hunters, creeping up on their prey very much like a house cat creeps up on a mouse.

Above: A female bighorn sheep and her kid.
Right: A cougar, also known as a mountain lion.

Below the sheep, at the foot of the mountain slope, is another herd, quietly grazing in a lush meadow. These grazers are the largest animals in Yellowstone: American bison.

A full-grown male bison, a bull, can weigh a ton, and its curved, sharp horns can be two feet long. Despite its weight, it can run up to forty miles an hour. Their thick, shaggy hair makes them look even

inside the animal's body by its fur, so none of it reaches as far as the snow on its back.

Winter can still be tough for bison, however. It's not the cold but the depth of the snow that's the problem. They can have a hard time reaching the grass that they need to eat, even when they use their big heads like snowplows to push the fluffy white flakes aside. Stored fat that they've put on over spring and summer,

Above: American bison in a grassy field.

Opposite: An American bison in Yellowstone National Park.

bigger. But the purpose of the hair isn't to make the bison look impressive; it's to keep the animal warm. The fur keeps in the heat of the animal's body, just like a thick winter coat keeps in the heat of your body. The bison's fur does such an incredible job of this that snow can settle on it without melting. The heat from the bison's skin is trapped

when grass is plentiful, helps them make it through the cold, dark, snowy winter. But sometimes that's not enough. Lack of food in winter is the biggest threat that a full-grown bison can face.

The herd below the eagle is a small one, just mothers and their calves. Each mother had one calf a few months ago, and now they stay close to their young ones, keeping an eye on their behavior and doing what bison spend most of their time doing— chewing. Like cows, bison are **ruminants**. This means they graze on grass and other plant life, and then they do something else— they chew their cud. After bison take a bite of grass, they swallow it, let it spend some time in a special part of their stomach called the **rumen**, and then spit it back up, or regurgitate it, into their mouths (now the grass is called a cud) for more chewing before it's swallowed again. Without the rumen and the bacteria that live there, breaking down the tough plant material that the bison swallows,

Sometimes American bison are called buffalo, but true buffalo have smaller heads, and have only thirteen ribs. The bison has fourteen.

**FASCINATING FACT**

Bison haven't always been the biggest animals in Yellowstone. Paleontologists (scientists who study fossils) found a plesiosaur fossil on a mountain in Yellowstone. This giant aquatic reptile lived in the seas during the age of the dinosaurs, more than 65 million years ago. Its discovery showed that Yellowstone was once underwater.

**FASCINATING FACT**

the bison couldn't get enough nutrition out of grass. (That's why human beings can't live off grass, by the way—we don't have a rumen to help us digest it.) It takes a lot of grass to keep a big animal like a bison alive, so bison spend a lot of their time eating fresh grass or chewing their cud.

As the eagle swoops overhead and the bison chew steadily away, an eerie sound echoes across the landscape below, a flat grassy valley with a river curling through it, the water gleaming silver in the last light of day. One low note rings out, then one higher, then another low, drawn-out note that seems to go on forever.

It's the howl of a single wolf. Then another joins in, and another, and the pups, who are just learning to howl, yip, and bark. It's dusk, and a wolf pack is gathering together to howl before setting out on a hunt.

If the bison hear it, they don't seem to

Above: Two wolves howling during a snowstorm.

Opposite: A large American bison.

react much—but they should be careful. A bison may be the largest animal in the park, but a wolf pack, working as a team, can sometimes attack a bison and bring it down.

In 1872, when Yellowstone became a national park, gray wolves were native there, along with other predators like bears and mountain lions. But most of the people who worked at the park or came to visit didn't like the idea of sharing their brand-new park with wolves. Wolves hunt animals like elk and deer, and a lot of the people in and around Yellowstone wanted to hunt those animals as well. Wolves also killed

and ate livestock—animals like cows and sheep that people were trying to raise. Get rid of the wolves, people thought, and cows could graze in safety. And there would be more big game for human hunters, too.

So wolves were hunted, shot, poisoned, and trapped. The last known wolf in Yellowstone National Park was killed in 1926; the last wolf in the Greater Yellowstone Ecosystem died in 1944.

But later people began to understand more about predators like wolves and what they do for an ecosystem. It turned out that wolves weren't bad for prey animals like elk—they were good for them. By hunting

Above: A wolf and her cubs at their den.
Opposite: A gray wolf crossing a river.

more wolves from a different part of Canada—British Columbia—came to the park.

None of those original wolves are alive today, but three hundred of their descendants live in the territories those first wolves chose within the Greater Yellowstone area. Half of them stay inside Yellowstone National Park itself, hunting and howling just like their ancestors did long ago.

Wolves live in packs, usually family groups. A pack is often a breeding pair, called an alpha male and female, and their pups. The alpha wolves are dominant over the others, which means that the others don't usually challenge them. They get the best chances to eat, mate, and have pups. After the pups grow up, they may travel out into the world to join other packs, or stay with their mother and father and brothers and sisters. The size of the packs in Yellowstone is constantly changing, as wolves die and are born, leave the pack, or are taken in. Some packs in Yellowstone have only two, three, or four wolves; others might have more than twenty.

The wolves in Yellowstone are gray wolves. (This is the name of their species and doesn't describe their color; most are gray, but they can be white or black.) They are about four and a half to six and a half feet long, and weigh anywhere between 55 and 130 pounds. They're not small animals, but they're nowhere near as big as an elk or a bison. They can run fast, too—about thirty miles an hour—but only for short distances.

elk, wolves keep the numbers of the herds down to where they're supposed to be. If elk aren't hunted, the herds get too big—and then there isn't enough food for each elk to eat. Without predators killing a few elk, a whole herd can starve.

Just being themselves and doing what they need to survive, wolves perform an important job to keep the ecosystem healthy. Each part of the ecosystem—the wolf hunting the elk, the bear eating the trout, the trout swimming upstream to spawn—is simply doing what comes naturally. But all these parts come together to make an ecosystem that works.

Once people figured this out, they decided to bring wolves back to Yellowstone. In March 1995, fourteen wolves were captured in Alberta, Canada, and taken to large pens in the park so that they could get used to their new home. They were released in April. A year later, seventeen

A pack of wolves.

So how can they catch such big prey?

The herd of elk that was grazing earlier in a clearing in the forest has come down to the river to drink and eat the lush grass there. But it might not have been the best choice for them. Several wolves from the pack have been stalking them for several minutes now. Like the mother grizzly, they're eager for the taste of meat. But unlike the grizzly, they can't turn to grass or berries or moths to ease their hunger if their hunt isn't successful. They need to make a kill.

Three wolves have carefully crept around the elk herd, getting into position. They've picked an old elk cow for their target. She's probably too old to bear calves anymore, and can't run as fast as a young elk. That makes her a wise choice for the wolves to try to take down.

One wolf springs out of the tall grass, dashing at the elk. Startled, she turns to flee toward her herd. But now there are two other wolves in front of her. The first wolf

A wolf's paw print is normally 4 1/2" long. A coyote's paw print is usually about 2" shorter.

has driven his prey toward the others, and now all three are chasing her.

If the elk turned and stood her ground, the wolves would probably back off. Her sharp hooves and powerful kicks would be too dangerous. A meal isn't worth getting killed for; it's better for a wolf to save its strength and stay uninjured for the next hunt.

But the cow doesn't turn and fight. She keeps running, and the wolves keep pace. One leaps and fastens his teeth in her hind leg. She shakes off the predator, but now she's wounded and bleeding, running more slowly. The other wolves draw in. More leap at her flanks and legs, nipping and biting. Each wound slows the elk even more.

The elk tries to turn, but her injured leg buckles under her. A wolf dodges in to grab her by the throat. She goes down, kicking and struggling, but in a few moments, it's over for her. The wolves eat eagerly, ripping open the cow's belly to get at the warm intestines, sometimes plunging their heads inside until they're bloody up to the eyebrows.

The wolves not only need to eat for themselves; they need to fill their stomachs with enough meat to bring some back for the pups still in the den. Once they reach

Notice the variety of colors in this group of gray wolves.

the den, the pups will lick the mouths of the hunters, who will obligingly bring some of the food, only partly digested, up from their stomachs for the little wolves to devour. When the pups are old enough, they'll join hunts like this, learning how to ambush prey, how to bring it down, how to make a kill so that the pack can survive.

It wasn't a good day for the elk cow. But her meat will nourish the wolf pack and feed the pups back at the den. And they aren't the only ones who will benefit. Only a few minutes after the elk cow is killed, ravens arrive to claim a share of the meat. Other scavengers—magpies, eagles, and foxes—will probably join them. Even a grizzly bear, wandering along, may feast on the wolf's kill. Insects will devour what's

Deer and elk horns are an important source of calcium for many of the animals that live in the forest.

they began to learn more about fire and what it does for an ecosystem.

The summer of 1988 was hot and dry. Less rain fell that summer than at any time in a hundred years. Conditions were just right for big fires—and big fires came. Most were natural, started by lightning, but two blazes were started by people. The biggest fire that summer began when someone dropped a lit cigarette. Overall, more than a million acres in Yellowstone National Park and the national forests around it burned.

Flames ripped through trees. Forests were reduced to smoky, ashy ruins. How could the plants and animals of Yellowstone's ecosystem survive? After the flames died down, people began to see how the ecosystem recovered. The fires actually turned out to be good for Yellowstone.

left. Rodents will chew on antlers and bones. Whatever isn't eaten will rot and nourish the soil. Grasses that the elk need to live, trees like aspen and cottonwood, and wildflowers like fringed gentian and shooting star will grow in the rich dirt. The energy that the cow gained for herself, grazing on the plants of Yellowstone, is fed back into the wolves that killed her, the scavengers that fed on her, the soil that her body enriched, and the plants that grew from that soil. Even in death, the elk cow is still part of the ecosystem.

Something else is part of the Yellowstone ecosystem, too. It's hard to imagine it on a peaceful evening, but twenty years ago, much of Yellowstone was in flames. For a long time, people thought of fire in the wilderness very much like they thought of wolves—something wild, dangerous, and savage, something that needed to be controlled or, even better, gotten rid of. But just as people learned more about wolves,

In an average year, about twenty-four fires (most small) are started by lightning in Yellowstone.

FASCINATING FACT

A fire may kill trees, but it doesn't destroy a forest. In fact, it makes it easier for new plants to grow. Big, old trees block the sunlight, so it's hard for shorter plants to grow under them. When these trees burn or fall in a fire, meadows are created where lots of sunlight can reach the ground. Seeds and roots in the ground survive the fire and send up new shoots. Other seeds are blown into the meadow by the wind or are brought in by animals. All the ash from burned wood fertilizes the ground, giving the new plants the nutrients they need to grow.

Fire can even help some trees plant new seeds. Many of Yellowstone's forests are lodgepole pine. A pine tree's seeds are deep inside its pinecones, and lodgepole

## FASCINATING FACT

The fire that swept through Yellowstone in 1988 was so hot that boulders exploded.

pine trees have two kinds of cones. One kind opens up during a normal year, letting the seeds inside drift to the ground. But the other kind of cone is sealed tight

A wildfire in the Bitterroot National Forest in Montana.

Left: Trees burned by a forest fire in Yellowstone surrounded by new life.

Above: A charred and open lodgepole pine cone.

with a sticky resin that dries as hard as rock. The only thing that can melt that resin is the heat of a forest fire. The same flames that burn a lodgepole pine to the ground open up its cones so that new seeds can take root. The old tree may die, but new ones will grow.

But what about animals? Fewer animals die in a forest fire than you might think. Most fires look terrible, but they don't move that fast. Animals can walk or run out of the way of the flames. Bird can fly. Rodents with burrows can escape underground. Some animals do die from breathing smoke, but not too many. And after the fire is gone, animals take advantage of the changes it brought to the forest.

Fire beetles are one species that find

fire useful. They look for charred wood to lay their eggs. Woodpeckers find a feast in a burned forest; the fallen trees are full of insects for them to eat. New meadows where trees are down create new hunting

Fire beetles look for charred wood to lay their eggs.

grounds for owls and hawks and delicious grazing for elk and deer. Hunters like wolves and bears and mountain lions prey on the **herbivores**, or plant eaters. The whole ecosystem benefits from the changes fire brings.

Fires happen in most years, but are usually small. A big fire like the one in 1988 is rare—one that size may happen every three hundred years. But big or little, fires are a natural part of Yellowstone's ecosystem. When humans tried to put out forest fires or keep them from starting, just as when they tried to kill all the wolves, they thought they were saving the rest of Yellowstone

from something that might hurt it. But we're learning that you can't change one part of an ecosystem without hurting another.

In an ecosystem, everything is connected. That's part of what the word *system* means. And every part of that system is important, even things that might seem fierce or dangerous or destructive. Wolves are a part of Yellowstone, just like elk. Fires are a part of Yellowstone, just like lodgepole pine. A predator that hunts and kills or a fire that burns a forest to ashes actually allows new life to grow. All the parts of an ecosystem need one another to survive.

A pair of elk.

# CALIFORNIA
# MONTEREY BAY
## The Golden State

**I**magine a forest where green, leafy fronds wave lazily underwater. Where fish and otters swim among towering seaweed the way birds fly among trees. This is the ecosystem that exists in the waters of the Monterey Bay.

Monterey Bay National Marine Sanctuary lies off the coast of central California. It was created by the United States government in 1992 to protect this diverse ecosystem.

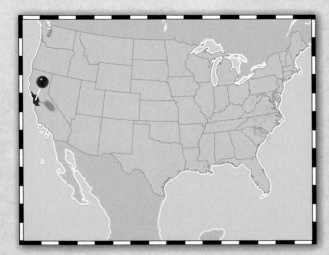

**Right: A variety of tide pool animals in Monterey Bay.**

Covering five-thousand, three hundred square miles of open water, it's larger than any national park on land in the United States, and it extends from the high-tide mark on the beach out to fifty-three miles offshore. The edge of the sanctuary that touches the shore makes up one-fifth of California's coastline.

In waters near the shore, sunlight filters down through strands of kelp. Cigar-shaped señorita fish dart past in bright flashes of orange. Bass kelp fish sparkle turquoise and

Top, right: Bull kelp up close.

Above: Waves breaking against rocks along the Monterey Bay shoreline.

Opposite: A sea bass swims through a kelp forest.

silver. A sea otter slips gracefully around the tall plants, a smooth, slippery dark shadow in a world of endless shades of green.

If you were swimming with this otter, you'd probably feel like you were diving among huge underwater trees. But even though kelp can look a lot like tall, slender, flexible trees, it's actually a very different plant. Kelp, which only grows underwater, is a type of algae, related to the colorful algae that grows in Yellowstone's hot springs or the green slime on the surface

There are two main kinds of huge kelp in the underwater forests of Monterey Bay. Giant kelp is a golden green color and has blades up and down the length of its stipe. It can live about seven years and can grow about ten or twelve inches a day. Giant kelp often grows to be 100 feet tall—even 175 feet, if the conditions are just right.

Bull kelp doesn't grow quite as tall as giant kelp, but considering that each plant lives only a year, its 60 feet is pretty impressive. Its long, thin blades, which take in the energy of the sun and gather nutrients from the water, grow only at the very top of its stipe. They trail through the water, looking a little like a bullwhip—which is where the plant got its name.

There may be as many as 500,000 creatures (some too small for the human eye to see) living on one giant kelp plant!

holdfast, like roots of a tree, keeps the kelp securely anchored to the ocean bottom.

Like all plants, kelp can turn sunlight into food. Energy from the sunlight, absorbed by the kelp's blades, allows it to combine water and carbon dioxide gas to make food for itself. The process is called **photosynthesis**. The nutrients that the kelp doesn't get from the sun, it absorbs from the water that surrounds it.

Life in Monterey Bay is dependent on the kelp that grows here. Most animals in the bay eat the kelp, or they eat the animals that eat the kelp. They use the kelp's blades to hide from predators, or they rely on the kelp forest as a good place to hunt.

And kelp doesn't only provide food and shelter while it's growing. Pieces of kelp are constantly being torn off by waves and currents, just like leaves drifting down from

of a pond. It has a **stipe**, a tall structure like a stem, and **blades**, or long fronds that drift with the movement of the water. Often the blades have floats, little bubbles filled with gas, that help keep them from sinking. A

A young harbor seal lying on a bed of kelp.

trees in a forest. These bits of kelp are so important to the ecosystem of Monterey Bay that they have their own name—**kelpshed**.

If kelpshed washes up on a sandy beach, it becomes food for plant eaters like sand flies and sandhoppers, tiny creatures that burrow in sand during the day and

A brightly striped jeweled top snail is one such grazer. It crawls slowly over a blade of giant kelp, using its tongue to scrape off the algae that clings to the kelp's surface. On the ocean floor, another type of snail, an abalone, is firmly anchored by its foot to a rock. It waits for a piece of kelp to tear

Above, left: A jeweled top snail crawling down the stipe of a giant kelp.
Above, right: A red turban snail.

come out to feed at night. If the floats on a blade of kelp are not broken, the kelp may drift at the water's surface, sometimes becoming entangled with other pieces to form wide, floating mats called paddies. Kelp paddies are used by fish and crabs for food and as places to hide from predators. Once the floats on a piece of kelpshed break, it drifts down into dark waters far from shore, becoming food for hungry deep-sea creatures like sea cucumbers or sea urchins.

But while kelp is still growing in the forest, it provides both food and shelter for an incredible number of animals. Some of these animals are grazers, feeding on the kelp itself or on the algae that grows on it.

A snail's tongue is called a radula. It has sharp, rasping edges like a file.

41

loose from the plant and drift down to it so that it can feed. Nearby, close to the kelp's holdfast, sea urchins are grazing, too.

Urchins love to graze on kelp. A sea urchin may not look like it has feet—or, really, many body parts at all—but it actually has tiny tube feet underneath its body, much like a sea star does. It can make its way along the bottom of the ocean, and when it comes across some kelp, it knows just what to do. An urchin has five teeth (also underneath its body), and it scrapes at the kelp, shredding it into tiny pieces and stuffing them into its mouth.

Mostly the urchin feeds on kelpshed. But if it finds a kelp holdfast, it will feed on that, too. If there are too many urchins grazing on kelp, they can actually do a lot of damage to a forest by eating away the holdfasts so that the plants come loose and drift away.

Fortunately, sea otters keep this from happening. Sea otters love to eat sea urchins. An otter, floating at rest on the water's surface, is now hungry, and she dives down to hunt. Her hind feet have webs between the toes and are flattened into a flipper shape, powering her through the water. Her keen eyes can see underwater as well as above, which helps her hunt for food. But she can also probe the ocean floor with her sensitive front paws, feeling for prickly urchins or other food—clams, abalone and other snails, crabs, sea stars.

She discovers a big purple sea urchin, but it's clinging firmly to a rock. If she grabs it too tightly, she risks getting painfully pricked by the urchin's long spines, so the otter picks up a rock and uses it to knock the urchin free. Then, holding the urchin delicately in her paws, she swims up toward the surface, using her foot-long tail to steer herself through the water.

A purple sea urchin growing among some coral.

On the surface of the water, the otter rolls over on her back, holding her prey, ready to eat. If she'd picked a hard-shelled animal like a clam, she might lay a flat rock on her chest like a dinner plate, place the clam on that, and smash the clam down to break it open. But an urchin isn't as tough. The otter breaks open its shell carefully with her paws, avoiding the long spines,

Above: A California sea otter floats in a kelp paddy in Monterey Bay.
Below: Purple sea urchins; a popular treat for otters!

and picks out the meat inside. She doesn't know it, but by catching and eating her favorite meal, she's helping to keep her ecosystem in check.

Once she's done with her meal, the otter begins to groom herself, running her paws through her dark fur. She has a flexible spine and loose skin. By twisting and turning and tugging at her skin, she can reach every inch of her coat to groom it, even the fur on her back.

The sea otter has the thickest fur of any mammal in the world—up to a million hairs per square inch. (Just to compare, most human beings have a hundred thousand hairs, not even close to a million, on their

You can easily tell if an otter's favorite food is purple sea urchins—its teeth turn purple!

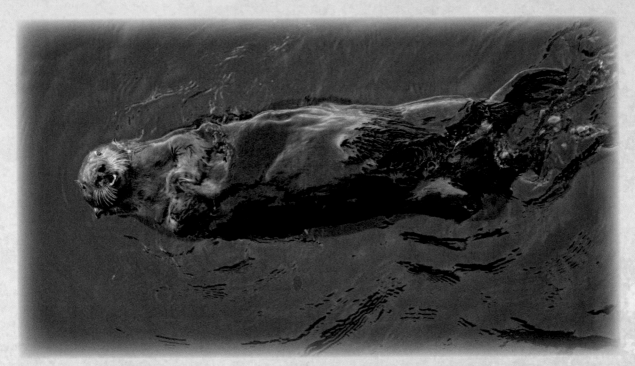

Above: A sea otter in Monterey Bay.
Opposite: A great white shark.

Sea otters have pouches made of loose skin where their front legs join the body. While hunting, they can stuff prey in the pouches and then hunt for more, coming back to the surface with a larger meal.

**FASCINATING FACT**

entire heads.) The otter needs this thick coat of fur to keep warm while swimming in the cold water of Monterey Bay, which doesn't get warmer than sixty-one degrees Fahrenheit at the surface, and about forty degrees deeper down. By grooming her coat, the otter is spreading oils from her skin through the fur. The fur becomes almost waterproof, and the cold water is kept away from the otter's skin. Tiny air bubbles also get trapped in the fur as the otter grooms it, and the bubbles act like insulation, forming a barrier that keeps in the warmth of her body.

The only parts of the otter's body that have no fur are her eyes, nose, mouth, and paws. That's why, when the otter is done grooming, she lifts her paws out of the water. It looks like she's waving to a friend, but actually she's keeping warm. More heat is lost in water than in air; if the otter left her paws in the water, she'd get cold faster.

Once she's done resting and grooming, the otter dives down into the water again to search for more food. This is the other way she stays warm in cold water—by eating. To keep her body warm, the otter burns the calories she gets from food. Sea otters spend a lot of time either hunting or bobbing on the surface to eat.

When the otter has captured and eaten enough sea urchins, she swims gracefully over to several other female sea otters at the surface. Otters hunt and eat alone, but when they're resting they usually keep close to other otters, in a group called a raft. Males raft with other males; females and young otters, called pups, raft together

as well. The female now settles down near the group and wraps a frond of kelp around herself for an anchor. After a brief rest, she'll probably return to the hunt.

The otter is a remarkable hunter, but she isn't the only predator in this ecosystem. Many hunters of prey, like seals, sharks, and octopuses, make the kelp forest their home, spending their lives among the blades or clustering on the ocean floor nearby.

Predators and scavengers come here to hunt for one simple reason—the kelp forest is full of food. The dense ocean plants slow down waves and currents, creating patches of calm water. These waters are perfect for young fish and **crustaceans** who aren't strong enough to survive rougher waters. Many of these animals use the kelp forests as a nursery; the young live and grow in the

quiet waters until they are old enough to head out into deeper waters on their own—or until they get eaten by a predator who's realized that a kelp forest is an excellent place to hunt.

One of those opportunistic scavengers, a decorator crab, creeps cautiously around the holdfast of a kelp plant. Its shell is covered—decorated—with bits of seaweed and tiny, living sea creatures: anemones that look like living flowers or creatures called bryozoans, which glue themselves to a surface like a kelp frond or a crab's shell and then create tiny boxlike shelters to hide in. All this decoration provides camouflage as the crab hunts for a meal, looking for small crustaceans or little sea sponges to snap up with its claws and stuff into its mouth.

When the decorator crab spies another hunter moving toward it across the ocean

Above: A juvenile sunflower sea star.
Opposite: A young decorator crab.

The decorator crab recycles its decorations. When it molts—sheds its old shell and grows a larger one—it carefully transfers the old decorations onto the new shell.

floor, it scrambles away as quickly as it can. The sunflower sea star started out life with only five arms, but now that it is an adult, it's grown twenty-four. All of those arms are covered with little tube feet—about fifteen thousand of them in all, to be exact. And those feet carry it along the ocean floor at the remarkable speed of forty inches per minute. The sunflower star's feet also help it hunt its prey: sea urchins, snails, sea cucumbers, crabs, even other sea stars.

Nibbling on a bit of kelpshed nearby is one of those prey animals: an abalone snail. It can't flee the sea star's approach as quickly as the decorator crab did. When the hunter's tentacles brush across it, the abalone twists its shell, hoping to break free. Then it tries to escape by moving as fast as it can,

Top: A juvenile leather star.

Middle: An abalone snail.

Bottom: A red sea star.

Top, right: A blood star in a typical kelp forest community.

oozing with its single, strong, muscular foot across the rocks. Unfortunately for the abalone, it's still a snail, and even moving at its fastest, it can't evade the sunflower star.

The star takes another grip on the abalone. This time its tube feet, like miniature suction cups, hold firm. The arms position the snail so that the opening of its shell is near the sea star's mouth, which is on the underside of the star's body, in the center of all its arms.

But the abalone is a big snail, too big to fit inside the sea star's mouth. That's not a problem for the sunflower star, though. Instead of getting the snail inside its stomach, it pushes its own stomach out of its mouth!

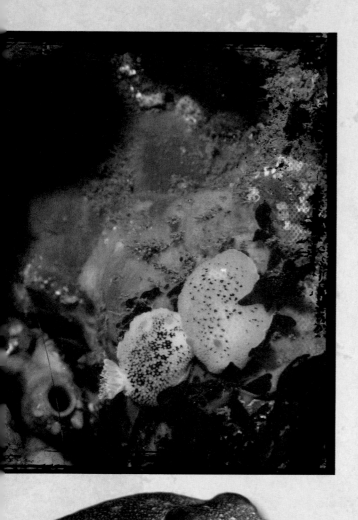

Then it forces the stomach inside the snail's shell. The sea star's stomach, now inside out, is covered with fluids that digest and break down prey. The fluids soon reduce the snail's body to a gooey soup, which is absorbed by the sea star's stomach. When the snail's shell is empty, the sea star swallows its stomach again and goes back on the hunt.

Near the sea star feasting on the abalone, piles of empty shells rest near a crack between two rocks. These shells tell of abalone and other snails who became food for a another predator of the kelp forest. Inside its den, a red octopus is resting. This **nocturnal** hunter doesn't venture out during the day, but at night it comes out of its den to look for prey like crabs, fish, and snails. Last night it collected several snails to bring back to its den. In addition to its eight tentacles, the octopus has a radula, just like a snail does, and it used this rough-edged tongue to bore a hole into the snails' shells. It injected a chemical into the shells that dissolved the snails into liquid, which the octopus could then slurp up. The snails' empty shells were then left outside its den with others that it had eaten, in a collection sometimes called an octopus's garden.

Octopuses are masters of disguise. A red octopus's skin is normally a reddish brown, but it can change to yellow, brown, red, white, or speckled patterns. It can blend in with its surroundings to hide from predators, or make itself stand out to attract a mate.

Not far from the octopus's garden, the sunflower star has finished its meal while a three-foot-long fish called a California sheephead is starting one. It has two long teeth that stick outside of its mouth like fangs, and it uses these to pry a sea urchin off a rock. Then it crunches its prey in its powerful jaws. Another big fish, a cabezon, rests quietly near the rocky bottom. So camouflaged that it looks like a rock covered with algae, the cabezon waits for prey—maybe a smaller fish—to come by. If something does swim within reach, the cabezon will burst out of hiding to gobble up its meal.

A señorita fish.

Yet another predator of the kelp forest swims overhead. This leopard shark is still young enough to be covered with the spots that give the species its name. Later, when it reaches its adult size, the spots will disappear and the shark will head out for deeper waters. But for now the coloration helps to camouflage the young shark as it hunts for fish, crabs, or other prey among the brownish-green strands of kelp.

Other species in the kelp forest rely on camouflage, too. A giant kelpfish would make an excellent meal for the young shark, but it's hoping to use camouflage to stay unnoticed. This might seem hard for

Above, left: A female California sheephead.
Above, right: A cabezon.

A leopard shark hunts in a kelp forest.

such a big fish—giant kelpfish can grow up to two feet long—but the kelpfish knows some tricks. Its body is shaped like a blade of kelp, and it sticks close to the kelp plants, looking like just another strand of seaweed. It can even change its color so that it blends in perfectly. It works—the leopard shark swims by without noticing the hidden fish.

Another fish, swimming by after the leopard shark has continued on its way, is not so lucky. The bright orange señorita fish is suddenly snatched up by a sleek, dark shape torpedoing down through the water. A strong beak snaps, and a pelagic cormorant, a bird about a foot and a half long, speeds back up to the surface with the fish in its beak. These birds are awkward fliers but graceful, agile swimmers and remarkable divers. They can go as deep as 180 feet, searching for fish and crabs.

The cormorant finishes the señorita fish and dives again. A kelp paddy nearby, floating on the water, bobs in the ripples created by the cormorant's dive. This little mat created from tangled bits of broken kelp makes a great spot for small animals

A cormorant dries its wings atop a buoy in Monterey Bay.

Above: A harbor seal swims through the water of Monterey Bay.
Left: A Madeira rockfish.
Opposite: A harbor seal basking in the sun.

like fish and crabs to hide from predators. A rockfish is hidden underneath, watching with its wide eyes for enemies and keeping an eye out for the smaller fish that it eats. Seeing one of those little fish come to the edge of the paddy to nibble at the kelp, it darts out to snatch up its prey in its teeth. But this turns out to be a mistake for the rockfish, because a larger predator is looming from below. A harbor seal, coming up after a deep dive, has its eye on a meal.

Like the sea otter, the harbor seal is a marine mammal. But it spends a little more time on land than the otter does. Otters sleep in the water and some even give birth to their pups there; seals drag themselves onto land (it's called *hauling out*) to rest, get warm, and have their babies.

On land, a harbor seal (like most seals) is slow and moves awkwardly, flopping along on its stomach. But in water it's quick and graceful. Its plump body, cushioned with a thick layer of fat under the skin to keep it warm, is streamlined and perfect for swimming. Its hind flippers move from side to side, pushing it forward; the seal steers with its front flippers.

The seal can see well underwater. Its eyes are protected from the salt water by a film of **mucus**. And the seal's long, sensitive whiskers also help it to find food,

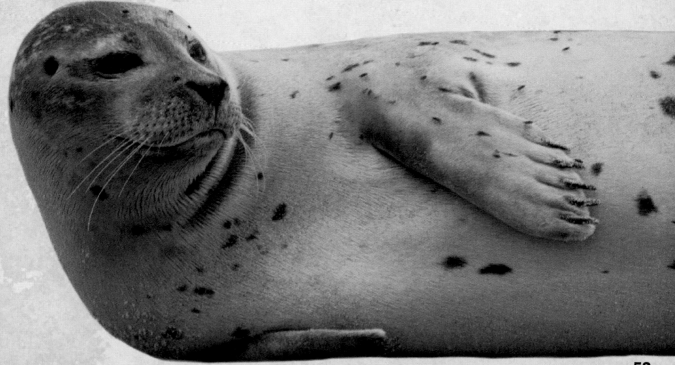

*The pattern of spots on each harbor seal's coat is unique. You can tell seals apart by looking at their spots.*

feeling the vibrations in the water, like the movement of a fish trying to escape.

The seal snaps up the rockfish, gulping it down headfirst, and stays at the surface for a minute or two. Then it opens up its nostrils to breathe before it dives again. Once it is underwater, its nostrils squeeze shut and its heart automatically slows down so that the oxygen in the seal's lungs will last longer. A harbor seal can stay beneath the water up to half an hour on a single breath.

As the harbor seal swims gracefully downward, it passes one of the bay's oddest-looking fishes—an ocean sunfish, also called a mola mola. The sunfish is one of

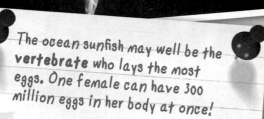

The ocean sunfish may well be the vertebrate who lays the most eggs. One female can have 300 million eggs in her body at once!

the world's biggest bony fish, weighing up to five thousand pounds! Only certain species of shark are bigger.

The giant fish looks like it is mostly made of a head, with a short tail attached directly to its head. Most fish move their tails from side to side to push themselves

forward in the water, but the sunfish's tail is too short. It flaps its fins to swim, and uses its tail to steer. It swims slowly, ignoring the harbor seal, who ignores it in turn.

Compared to the harbor seal, the sunfish is a slowpoke. But it can swim fast enough to catch up to the comb jelly that it's pursuing. Unlike many jellies that have tentacles, this beautiful, shimmering jelly moves by beating eight rows of comblike plates, rowing itself through the water. The sunfish slowly but surely bears down on it, opens its mouth, and captures the jelly,

**FASCINATING FACT** A jelly's body is about 95 percent water; it has no bones, shell, heart, or even brain.

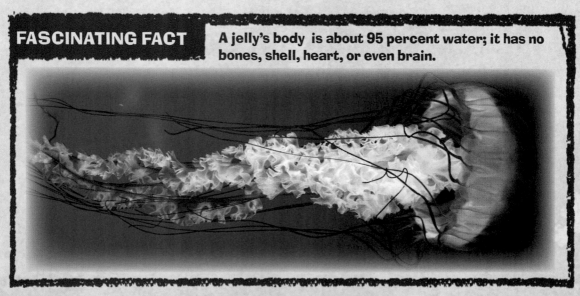

holding it firmly in its sharp teeth. Then the sunfish sucks water into its mouth and spits it out. The force of the water shooting out of the fish's mouth shreds the fragile jelly into pieces that the sunfish can swallow.

The harbor seal, meanwhile, is hunting for more fish, not realizing that another predator is lurking below. Silently, a male killer whale, or an orca, rises up toward the seal.

An orca is one of the smartest and deadliest hunters in the ocean. Sleek, fast swimmers, they hunt a wide variety of prey, everything from salmon to sharks to blue whales. And this particular orca has a seal dinner on his mind.

Male orcas can grow up to thirty feet, but this one is smaller. He's young, which may be why he's on his own. Orcas live in pods, groups that can be as small as two or three animals or as large as fifty. Some orcas spend all their lives with the pod they were born into; others may leave when they grow up and travel by themselves

Opposite, left: An ocean sunfish, also known as a mola mola.
Opposite right: A colorful luminescent jellyfish.
Above: An orca uses its strong tail to leap out of the water of Monterey Bay.

Above: A pod of orcas, easily recognized by their distinctive dorsal fins.

Opposite: A young harbor seal along the rocky shore of Monterey Bay.

for a while before finding a new pod to join. Maybe this young male is on such a journey.

The whale puts on a burst of speed, opening his mouth, and the seal realizes it's in danger. It zigzags frantically away, and the whale's mouth snaps shut on nothing but water. Immediately he changes direction to chase the seal.

Darting and dodging, the seal flees toward the surface of the water. The whale, swimming faster, closes the gap. This time he keeps his mouth closed and tries to ram the seal with his head. If he succeeds, he could knock the seal right out of the water, and the stunned, disoriented mammal would be easy prey after it fell back in.

But the seal dodges again, and the whale misses once more. The speed of

his charge carries him right past his prey. Quickly, before turning around, he smacks the seal with his powerful tail. Stunned, the seal tumbles over in the water, and the whale swivels around, his mouth open again.

But the whale has accidentally knocked the seal into just the right place—toward a rocky ledge that juts out of the water. The seal is dazed and battered, but it manages to scramble onto the rocks. The frustrated whale circles the ledge several times, his tall black **dorsal** fin sticking out of the water. He finally swims off, looking for other prey.

The orca may not have gotten a meal, but he did get something else—a lesson about which hunting tactics work best. Hopefully this knowledge will be useful

the next time he needs to hunt down a meal. And maybe the seal has learned to stick closer to shelter like the rocky ledge, where it can find safety from hungry predators. Predator and prey, both trying to survive, end up teaching each other lessons about the perils of life in the ecosystem of the Monterey Bay.

The seal was lucky, though, that it faced only a single orca. If it had been trying to escape from an entire pod, it might not have lived long enough to learn any kind of lesson. When a pod hunts as a group, it can be very hard for prey to escape. Sometimes a pod works together to circle a school of fish, forcing them into a tight ball, and then smacks the school with their tails, stunning or killing fish that they can then pick up later. Sometimes a pod attacks a much bigger whale, chasing it for hours to tire it out, biting and slashing at its sides to weaken it, and even leaping on top of it to force it underwater, trying to keep it from taking a breath. Some orcas have even learned to use bait to lure in their prey. They will spit out partially digested food to float on the surface of the water, and then wait underneath. When seagulls fly down to the water to eat the food that the orca has thrown up, the orca surges up to catch the bird.

All of these clever tactics not only get the whales the food they need to survive, they keep the ecosystem healthy by making sure that the numbers of prey animals—seals, fish, otters, or even seagulls—are kept in control. Just like the wolves in Yellowstone or the insect-eating bats of the Sonoran Desert, orcas help keep their ecosystem in balance.

Would you be surprised to learn that you're a part of the Monterey Bay ecosystem, just like an otter or an octopus? Like so many of the creatures in Monterey Bay, you depend on kelp for your food, even if you don't know it. Look at the label on your favorite brand of ice cream, or your cereal, or your toothpaste. Do you see the word *algin*? Then you're a part of the kelp food chain! Algin is used to thicken creamy food like ice cream, and it's made from kelp. The ecosystem that begins with the kelp forest reaches up onto sandy beaches, down into deep underwater canyons, and into your kitchen as well.

Opposite: A kelp forest.

Above: An orca breaks the surface of the water at sunset over Monterey Bay.

Below: A common seagull.

As the young male orca swims off, the waves created by his powerful tail wash through a nearby kelp paddy, tearing off small pieces of kelp. One of those pieces starts to drift slowly down into the water. After a while the piece of kelpshed is three hundred feet deep. At this depth, the water around it is getting colder, and the light is dimming. It's too dark for plants to grow down here.

Left: Feather stars.

Above: Bioluminescent jellies in the deep waters of Monterey Bay.

Plants turn the sun's energy into food; animals then eat the plants, turning the plant's energy into food for themselves. Without sunlight, this kind of **food chain** cannot exist. How can life survive in waters that are too deep and dark to allow plants to grow?

Plants may not be able to grow below three hundred feet, but pieces of broken plants do sink to the bottom. The piece of kelp blade that is drifting down will be food for any herbivore that encounters it. The water near the surface is also full of plankton, tiny plants and the tiny swimming creatures that eat them. Some of this plankton—either dead or alive—drifts down alongside the kelpshed. These two things, plankton and kelpshed, are the basis for most of the food chains that support the deep-dwelling animals of Monterey Bay—shrimp and krill, jellies and squid, worms and crabs, sharp-toothed fish with giant mouths, and many more species that scientists have yet to discover.

The piece of kelp that was torn off the paddy continues to sink. Deeper than two thousand feet, it drifts alongside a creature that's related to both jellies and coral—a giant siphonophore. This remarkable creature, mostly transparent, more than a hundred feet long but only about as big around as a broom handle, is actually a colony of several individuals, all performing specialized jobs. One might sting prey to death, another might digest it, and yet another helps the siphonophore swim. The individuals spend their lives attached to make up the big animal. No single one could survive on its own.

**FASCINATING FACT**

The biggest siphonophore ever discovered was longer than a blue whale!

Above: A siphonophore.
Below: A yellow anglerfish.

The bit of kelp drifting past isn't food for the giant siphonophore, which is hunting for small crustaceans and jellies. But the siphonophore does react to the kelp. When the plant brushes against it, the creature does something incredible—it lights up, glowing a bright blue.

Many of the creatures who live in deep, dark waters are **bioluminescent**—able to create their own light—like fireflies. But bioluminescence is more common in water

Pickup Before: 2/9/2015

# LOTHAMER

3577

A gulper eel can unhinge its jaw and stretch out its stomach so that it can swallow a fish as big as itself.

**FASCINATING FACT**

than on land. The light inside the bodies of bioluminescent animals like the siphonophore can be used by an animal to lure in food, to confuse a predator, or to signal to other creatures who may become its mate.

As the glowing siphonophore swims along, a tiny tadpole snailfish, only a few inches long, darts away from the big predator. Then something else catches the little fish's attention. It swims off to investigate a tiny light that seems to bob and float in the darkness. This is a mistake. The snailfish is getting closer and closer to a hunter that bristles with spiny fins. The fanfin anglerfish can't see the snailfish; there's not enough light down here for it to see by. But with its long fins, it feels

An artist's rendering of the little-seen anglerfish.

the vibrations in the water caused by the swimming snailfish. It waits and waits until the fish comes closer. Hanging in the water over the anglerfish's head is something that looks like a long, bony pole. The tip glows with bioluminescent light, luring in unwary prey like the snailfish, who is snapped up in one bite.

Far below the anglerfish, at six thousand feet, a gulper eel swims along. This creature's enormous mouth seems too large for its slender body, and too large for the small fish it usually finds to eat. But the eel's big mouth allows it to eat just about any animal it comes across, and that's an advantage in these deep waters, where food is scarce.

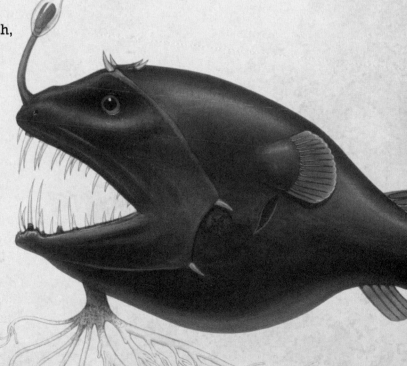

Even deeper, at a little more than ten thousand feet, is the floor of Monterey Canyon, the deepest point in the Monterey Bay National Marine Sanctuary. This cold, dark world couldn't seem more different from the sunny, life-filled waters of the kelp forest. No light at all reaches this deep. It's about forty degrees Fahrenheit. And the weight of ten thousand feet of water is crushing. But life finds a way to survive here.

Like all living things, the creatures that live in the depths of Monterey Bay need something to provide them with food. Long ago, an orca died and its corpse drifted down through the water. It came to rest here, on the canyon floor. Its flesh has long since been eaten or rotted away. Only the bones are left—but those bones are nourishing new life.

Above: A blue whale leaps out of the water.

Below: A blue whale swims in the deeper water of Monterey Bay.

A variety of corals and sponges in Monterey Bay.

Two species of tube worms, called whale worms, have been discovered living on the deep-sea floor of Monterey Bay, eating the bones of whales. Whalebones contain a huge amount of oil, which is what the worms are feasting on. A single whale carcass, called a **whalefall**, can support a whole population of worms.

The worms do not have eyes, legs, mouths, or even stomachs. They have feathery red plumes that stretch out into the water and act like **gills**, drawing in oxygen. The plumes are attached to a long, slender body; the other end of the body is buried inside the whalebone itself. Inside the

bone the worm has a sac full of eggs and also green tendrils that look like roots. The tendrils reach deep into the bone. Bacteria live inside the tendrils, and the bacteria break down the fat and oil contained in the whalebone to provide food for the worms.

The worms will live on the whalebones until the entire skeleton has been eaten.

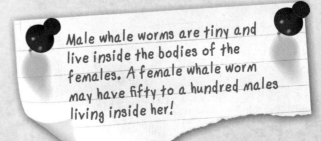

Male whale worms are tiny and live inside the bodies of the females. A female whale worm may have fifty to a hundred males living inside her!

Then they will all die. But before they die, they send their fertilized eggs or larva—the young form of a whale worm—out into the water. Most of the eggs or larvae won't survive. But some may reach a new whale-fall. There they will grow into worms that

Above: A bed of vesicomyid clams on the floor of Monterey Bay.
Opposite: A section of Monterey Bay shoreline.

will continue to eat until the new carcass has been devoured.

Like whalebones, **cold seeps** are another source of life in the deep ocean. In three places inside the Monterey Bay Sanctuary, liquid seeps out of cracks in the seafloor. This fluid is rich in a chemical called sulfide. Sulfide is poisonous to most animals, but not to the creatures like vesicomyid clams who live on a cold seep. They depend on bacteria that can change the sulfide into food.

Clams living in the mud have these bacteria inside their bodies, just as whale worms have bacteria inside their tendrils. The clams draw the sulfide into their bodies; the bacteria change the sulfide into food for the clam. The clam gets nutrients; the bacteria get a home. Other creatures like worms, mussels, snails, and crabs may depend on the bacteria at a cold seep, too. Hunters like Dover sole and octopuses can come by to feed there.

Every ecosystem needs a source of energy. The sunlight falling on the blades of a kelp forest is one kind of energy, the kind that supports most life on Earth. The sulfide seeping out of the seafloor is another. Life in Monterey Bay, and all over the planet, finds a way to take the energy that comes into its ecosystem, convert it into food, grow, and live. The ways that living creatures connect and interact as the energy in a blade of kelp is transferred from an urchin to an otter, or the energy in sulfide moves from bacteria to a clam to an octopus, is part of what makes an ecosystem so fascinating—and so fragile.

**FASCINATING FACT**

Some of the clams who live on the sulfide in Monterey Bay can take a century to grow into adults.

If any one part of an ecosystem is changed or disrupted, the energy cannot flow from one living thing to another as it should. If the waters of Monterey Bay become clouded with dirt or pollution, then the energy of the sunlight cannot reach the kelp as it should. All of the creatures of Monterey Bay who depend on the kelp can suffer. Or if oil from a tanker ship spills into the water, it can kill otters, who can't clean the oil out of their coats. A dirty coat won't keep an otter warm; it will freeze to death. Without otters to control the population of sea urchins, the urchins may eat away at the kelp forests until they disappear— and again, the whole ecosystem of Monterey Bay will be damaged.

Since Monterey Bay is a marine sanctuary, its waters and the creatures that live there are protected. It's against the law to dump trash or to drill for oil here. There are rules about how many and what kinds of fish can be caught. But all the world's oceans are connected, and what people do outside of the boundaries of the Monterey Bay National Marine Sanctuary can change the bay's ecosystem. We're just beginning to understand the complex ecosystems of the oceans, and how our actions can affect them. The more we learn, the more we understand how careful we must be so that human activity doesn't harm delicate and complex ocean ecosystems like Monterey Bay.

# THE SONORAN DESERT

**I**magine a desert that stretches over one hundred thousand square miles, that reaches into five states and two countries. That's the Sonoran Desert. This dry land is home to towering saguaro cacti and scrubby sagebrush, to coyotes and Gila monsters and desert tortoises. It makes up part of two American states (California and Arizona) and three Mexican ones (Sonora, Baja California Norte, and Baja California Sur).

Right: A variety of cactus and other plants in the Sonoran Desert.

But what is a desert? A desert can be hot or cold, high in the mountains or down low, sandy or full of plant life, but one thing makes it a desert: it's dry. A desert is a place where very little rain falls. When rainstorms do come, they are unpredictable; some years there may be no rain at all. Every living thing in a desert ecosystem, whether it's a plant or an animal, has to find some way to survive without much water and to live through times of drought.

In the hottest, driest areas of the Sonoran Desert, like the lower Colorado River Valley, the temperature in summer can reach 120 degrees Fahrenheit, and the soil can be 180 degrees—hot enough to burn your feet. In these parts of the desert, fewer than three inches of rain falls most years. In other parts of the Sonoran, storms in the rainy seasons can bring a foot of rain a year. These rains are sudden and heavy,

The Arctic and the Antarctic are considered deserts because so little rain or snow falls there.

but they don't last long, and the desert quickly returns to its dry state.

Despite these dry and oftentimes harsh conditions, many living creatures thrive. There are 2,000 species of plants in the Sonoran Desert, 350 species of birds, and 60 species of mammals. And they have all evolved to fit perfectly in the desert; some couldn't live anywhere else.

One of those mammals is the coyote. This small, scrappy member of the dog family lives in prairies, mountains, forests, and even in cities, where it hunts small animals and raids garbage cans. Wherever a

Top: A horned toad.
Middle: A trio of young burrowing owls.
Bottom: A sleeping rattlesnake in the Sonoran Desert.
Left: Clouds build over the Sonoran Desert.

coyote can find a meal, it can make a home. And coyotes are very much at home in the Sonoran Desert.

One coyote there is looking for food. His tawny brown fur blends into a background of dry grasses and sunbaked dirt, making him hard to see as the daylight starts to fade. About twenty pounds, this male coyote is a year old. He was born last spring, and has lived with his mother and father ever since.

Like wolves, many coyotes live in packs. A pack is often one family, a mother and father and their children, some grown up and others still pups. This coyote was one of a litter of six. Four of his littermates headed out on their own once they were big enough, but he and one of his sisters stayed with his parents' pack. Now they're helping to raise a new litter of pups.

The pups are still at the den, being watched by their mother, while the other members of the pack hunt. If the coyotes were chasing large prey, they might work as a team, as wolves often do. But if they are after small prey, coyotes often hunt alone.

The coyote pokes his black nose into a tangle of brush, sniffing hard. His large, triangular ears twitch. Smell and hearing are the senses that the coyote relies on most when he's searching for a meal. A coyote will eat almost anything—mice, rats, birds, snakes, eggs, berries, fruit, grass, and even roadkill. And something in this brush has caught his attention.

Left: A young coyote.
Right: A mature coyote.

The coyote jumps back when the brush rustles. A large, scaly reptile with pinkish-orange and black stripes—a Gila (pronounced *hee*-lah) monster—is making its way out of its **burrow**, the hole in the ground in which it spends most of its time.

Living in a burrow is one way to survive in the desert. In a place where the air can get to be more than one hundred degrees Fahrenheit and the surface of the ground much hotter than that, an underground burrow stays nice and cool, between sixty and seventy degrees. That's good for a Gila

monster, which is cold-blooded, like other reptiles. That means it can't control its body temperature for itself. If the air around it or the ground under it is hot, the Gila monster gets hot. If its surroundings are cold, the Gila monster is cold. So it stays in a cool underground burrow on scorching days and searches out the sun if it gets chilly in winter. The Gila may spend up to 98 percent of its life underground. It could survive in its burrow for up to a month if it had to, living off water stored in its bladder and the fat in its body and its thick tail.

In addition to staying in its burrow, the Gila monster uses another tactic to survive in the desert heat. It usually comes out at night, when the temperatures are cooler.

Many desert species do this, too, including the coyote; they are sometimes active in the day, but prefer to rest in the heat and search for food at night, dawn, or dusk. Now, since the evening is starting to fall and temperatures have become comfortable, the Gila monster is ready to step out of its hole, only to encounter a coyote with dinner on its mind.

And this coyote is a good deal bigger than the Gila monster, which is about a foot and a half long. Even so, the coyote doesn't pounce on the Gila, and the Gila doesn't try to scuttle back underground. Instead, the Gila monster opens its mouth wide, lets out a loud hiss, and backs up a few steps. But it's not trying to run away. It's making a threat display, warning the coyote to back off—or else! The coyote hesitates, then trots away, making a wide circle around the lizard.

An old superstition about Gila monsters claimed that once they bite, they can't let go until sundown. It's not true; the Gila doesn't care whether or not the sun has set. But it definitely bites hard and holds on!

Maybe the coyote has encountered a Gila monster before, and learned from its mistake. The Gila is one of only two venomous lizards in the world. It has **glands** that produce venom in its lower jaw, and when it bites, a Gila monster clamps its jaws down hard and chews, forcing the venom deep into the wound.

Opposite: A Gila monster preys on some desert quail eggs.
Top: A Gila monster.

A Gila monster's bite probably wouldn't be fatal to a human, but it is terribly painful. It causes swelling, nausea, and vomiting. The coyote was wise not to try to take on the Gila. There are less risky ways to find a meal.

The Gila monster continues slowly across the Sonoran landscape. Just like the coyote, it's searching for food. Its tongue flicks in and out of its mouth. Like a snake, the Gila can pick up smells with its tongue. And it seems to have found something, because it stops at a small hollow in the ground and begins to dig.

After a few minutes of digging with its sharp front claws, the Gila comes across six round eggs, buried about half a foot deep. Six months ago, a desert tortoise dug this hole with her back legs and laid her eggs, then covered them up and went on her slow way. Now these eggs are a meal for the Gila monster, who breaks open each one and licks out the inside. To make up for days or even weeks when it stays in its burrow and doesn't eat at all, the Gila

Above: A Gila monster basks on a rock.

Opposite: A desert tortoise.

gorges when it finds food, swallowing as much as possible.

The protein-rich eggs are good for the Gila monster, but bad for the young tortoises who will never hatch. However, even if they *had* hatched, the chances of the tortoises making it to adulthood would have been low. Coyotes and badgers will both happily make a meal out of a young tortoise. Out of every one hundred tortoise eggs laid, only a few will grow up to lay eggs of their own.

The female tortoise who laid these eggs did not stay around to protect them from the Gila monster or any other predators. But she's probably not too far away, either. Tortoises don't roam much; most spend their lives within a few miles of the place where they were hatched.

Like the Gila monster, the desert tortoise has adapted to the heat of a desert ecosystem by spending much of its time underground. Its front legs are flattened, and good for digging. In the nearby Mojave Desert, tortoises dig deep burrows—sometimes they go on for thirty-five feet!—and more than one tortoise may live there. In the Sonoran, though, desert tortoises live alone. Burrows here may be just deep enough for one tortoise to get inside.

In winter, a tortoise hibernates in its burrow. In summer, it does something similar—it **estivates**. During estivation, the tortoise stays underground, not eating, not moving. It lives on water stored in its bladder, and its body can even absorb some minerals from its shell to keep itself going. Estivation helps the tortoise survive hot weather and drought, just as hibernation helps it survive the cold. When it's not too

When male tortoises fight over mates, each tries to use an extension called a gular horn on his bottom shell to flip the other over.

**FASCINATING FACT**

hot or too cold, mostly in spring and fall, tortoises crawl out of their burrows to find the food and water they need to survive.

The tortoise who laid the eggs is out of her burrow right now and feasting on a delightful tortoise treat—the bright red fruit of the prickly pear cactus. Just like the tortoise, the Gila monster, and other desert animals, the cactus has to find a way to survive in a dry environment. Cacti like the prickly pear

Above: A pair of javelinas.
Left: A prickly pear cactus bearing fruit.

have thick, waxy skin that holds in water, and large cells inside the plant can store water for times when no rain falls.

The tortoise is intent on getting as much fruit into her stomach as she can. Like all turtles, the tortoise has no teeth; she stretches her neck to seize the fruit in her beaklike mouth, mashes it up, and then uses her tongue to push the pulp back toward her throat. Tortoises aren't the only animals who stuff themselves when the prickly pear fruit ripens. Rabbits, pack rats, javelina, deer, squirrels, birds, cactus beetles, and even humans all eat the juicy red fruit, gaining valuable moisture as well as calories.

And it isn't only the animals who benefit when they eat the prickly pear's fruit. These animals swallow the seeds along with the fruit, and later, when they get rid of their body's waste, the seeds can take root in the ground and grow new plants. The animals get food and help spread the plant seeds through their digestive process. The plants are then able to grow in many different places. Each living thing, simply trying to do what it needs to—eat enough to survive or scatter seeds so more plants can grow—contributes to the health of the desert ecosystem.

The prickly pear fruit that the tortoise is eating is growing from a pad, or a flattened part of the stem, where there's a fluffy white spot that looks like mold. Tiny insects called cochineals live hidden under the white fluff. When female cochineals are young, they crawl to the edge of the cactus pad where they were hatched. Their bodies produce long, waxy white strands, and, when the wind picks these up, they are blown to a

The color of cochineal insects has made them valuable to people over the years. Female cochineals are a dark, deep red. When their bodies are dried and ground up, they make a dye that can be used to color cloth. When Europeans first discovered this dye, it was rare and expensive. You would have had to be very rich to own a cloak or a dress colored with dead insects. In fact, in some countries, only the king was allowed to wear cochineal red or crimson.

Cochineal dye is still used today. But you're more likely to discover it not in the clothes you're wearing, but in the food you're eating. It's most common in candy and drinks. Look at the ingredients list on red candy, cherry soda, or fruit punch. If you see "cochineal" or "carmine," you're probably eating insects like the ones who found a home on the prickly pear cactus!

Ancient cacti once had leaves, but over millions of years, the leaves evolved into the plant's spines.

**FASCINATING FACT**

Opposite: Mature saguaro cacti.

Above: Quail eggs in a nest.

Right: A Gila woodpecker feeding on a saguaro cactus.

the plant is tall. The folds in the cactus's skin expand as the tissues inside become plump and full of water. After a good rain, about 90 percent of a saguaro's weight can be the water it has absorbed.

If it gets enough water, the saguaro grows quickly. With little rain, its growth is slow. In a more moist area, a saguaro may reach eight feet tall—the height at which it usually starts to bloom—in forty years. In a dry area, it may take it seventy-five years to get that tall. But a saguaro has plenty of time. Most live to between 150 and 175 years old; some even live to 200!

In all of those years (and even after they've died) saguaros provide benefits to the desert ecosystem. Like the prickly pear, the saguaro cactus bears a red, juicy fruit. This fruit gets ripe in June or July, the driest months of the year. At that time, it's the only source of moisture that many animals can get, and they eat it eagerly.

And birds also use the saguaro to nest in, just like birds in other habitats use trees. Building nests off the ground helps keep eggs and hatchlings safe from predators, and the saguaro's spines add extra protection for birds like the Gila woodpecker. These woodpeckers carve out a

new cactus pad. They settle down, lose their legs, and attach themselves by their mouths to the new pad. Then they cover themselves with a fluffy white material that they make  inside their own bodies; it protects them from predators and the harsh desert sun. They will stay attached to that cactus pad for the rest of their lives.

Not too far from the prickly pear is another remarkable cactus of the Sonoran Desert—the saguaro. This giant desert plant is the tallest cactus in the desert, and can easily reach forty feet.

The saguaro cactus is a master at using whatever water comes its way in the dry desert environment. Like the prickly pear, it has a thick skin that keeps any moisture inside from being lost. This skin has pleats, or folds, that run up and down the plant from top to bottom. After a rain, the saguaro absorbs all the moisture it can through its roots, which spread out around it as far as

Above: A kestrel.
Below: A sidewinder rattlesnake.
Opposite: Mature saguaro cacti.

deep cavity in the saguaro in which to nest. They make new nests each spring, and other birds, like elf owls, house finches, and kestrels, come along to put the old nests to good use. Even once saguaros have died and fallen to the ground, they can still offer a home for snakes, rodents, and lizards, who hide underneath them or burrow inside. All its life and even after it dies, the saguaro supports and shelters other living things, playing an important role in the ecosystem.

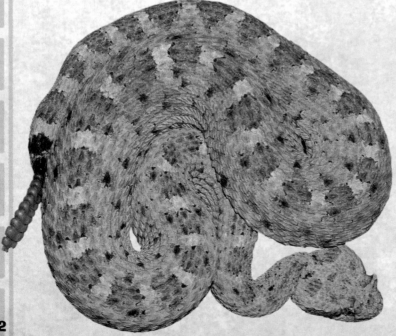

**FASCINATING FACT**

The tallest saguaro cactus ever measured was seventy-eight feet!

82

A coyote stands on a rock in the early morning sunlight.

The young male coyote who was hunting earlier now comes trotting across the desert, pausing at the base of the saguaro to sniff hopefully for anything that could be prey. The Gila monster didn't turn out to be a good target, and the coyote hasn't found anything else to fill his stomach. He's still searching. His ears swivel toward a sound in a patch of grass; his nose twitches. Something in that patch of grass may be the meal he's been hoping for.

The coyote creeps forward as quietly as he can. Then he stands still, stiff-legged, listening carefully. He doesn't want to frighten away the prey. Finally he pounces, making a little hop and coming down with both front paws together. But he missed and his prey, a band-winged grasshopper, leaps away. With its powerful legs, a grass-

## FASCINATING FACT

Coyotes can breed with both domesticated dogs and wolves. A dog with one coyote parent and one dog parent is called a coydog.

hopper can jump twenty times its body length. Imagine watching a person leap over one hundred feet! And the grasshopper has another trick in store that might help it escape from the coyote's jaws.

It's in the air now, and both pairs of wings are open. The dull brown forewings are not used for flight; they just cover up the back wings, which help the grasshopper make its astonishing leap. The back wings also have bright orange bands. The coyote's eye follows this spot of bright color through the air. But then, as the grasshopper lands, it covers up its back wings with the forewings. Instantly the bright orange spot has vanished, and the insect blends in perfectly with the dusty ground. The coyote can't see it anymore; for the moment, the insect is safe.

But the grasshopper wasn't alone. Several more leaped out of the grass when the coyote pounced, and the coyote didn't lose sight of them all. He jumps again, and this time pins down his prey before it can leap away. A quick snap of the jaws, and the coyote has a struggling grasshopper in his mouth.

With a couple of bites, the coyote swallows the grasshopper and goes after another. Full of protein, grasshoppers can make a good meal—if the coyote can get enough of them into his mouth. But the coyote stops chasing the insects to look around. Something else has caught his eye, or maybe a

new scent has crossed his sensitive nose. The grasshopper took the edge off his hunger, but he wouldn't say no to a larger meal. And what he can smell now might be just that.

Above: A band-winged grasshopper.
Below: Creosote bushes.

The coyote's attention is on a creosote bush, a scrubby plant about four feet tall, with small dark green leaves at the ends of thin branches. No sound or movement comes from the bush, but the coyote's nose

tells him that an antelope jackrabbit is hiding there. The jackrabbit knows very well that the coyote is nearby. When the coyote pounced on the grasshopper, it stood up on its back legs to its full height, about two feet, to see its enemy more clearly. Now it's huddled close to the ground, perfectly still, hoping that the coyote will pass it by.

The antelope jackrabbit is not actually a rabbit, despite the confusing name. It's a hare. Hares are larger than rabbits—the antelope jack is four or fives times as big as a more common cottontail rabbit.

Jacks can run faster than rabbits, too, and this jack will need to rely on its swift-

Above: An antelope jackrabbit, alert for predators.
Below:  A black-tailed jackrabbit in the shade of a rocky outcrop.
Opposite: A coyote howls in the twilight in the Sonoran desert.

ness very shortly. The coyote is getting too close. With a sudden burst of speed, the jack leaps out of the creosote bush and dashes away, covering fifteen feet with one leap. The coyote is after it instantly. A big antelope jack would be a magnificent meal.

But it'll be hard work to catch it. The jack doesn't have a burrow to flee to, like a rabbit does. During the heat of the day, it simply finds some shade to rest in or settles into a patch of grass or weeds. It relies on its speed to outrun predators that it can't hide from. By now it is leaping at thirty-five miles an hour. This isn't a short sprint, either, that will leave the hare exhausted and easy for the coyote to catch. The jack can keep up this pace for half a mile if it has to.

The antelope jackrabbit quickly switches

direction, zigzagging across the dusty ground. In the dim twilight, patches of white fur on each flank flash, just like those of a pronghorn antelope, which is where the hare got its name. The coyote follows, but he loses time on each turn. The jack gains ground, and shortly the coyote gives up, letting his prey bound away.

The moon rises over the horizon as the coyote sits back on his haunches to release a brief howl, letting the other members of his pack know where he is and listening

Top: A lesser long-nosed bat eating pollen from a cactus.
Above: A California leaf-nosed bat.

for their response. Another howl, not too far away, answers him, and the coyote trots toward the sound, heading back to the den. The grasshopper wasn't much of a meal, but perhaps he'll find a few more on his way back to join his pack.

As the coyote makes his way home and the sky darkens, a new kind of hunter ventures outside and swoops across the sky. The California leaf-nosed bat is on the wing and looking for prey.

There have been bats on Earth for 50 million years, and in that time they have spread to every continent except Antarctica, changing and adapting to different environments all over the planet. There are bats with wingspans six feet across. Others

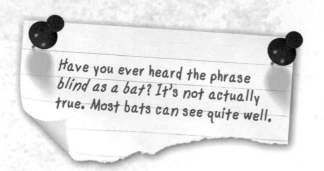

are so small they weigh less than a penny. Some bats eat fruit, while others sip nectar from flowers or hunt lizards, frogs, small rodents, birds, minnows, and even other bats. And there are actually bats that drink blood. (Yes, vampire bats truly do exist!) The California leaf-nosed bat, however, is hunting for insects, as many bats do. And it's very well adapted to finding them.

This bat has amazing ears, one inch long, about a third as long as its body. (Imagine if your ears reached from the top of your head to the middle of your chest!) With these ears, it can hear a cricket's footsteps or a caterpillar chewing. And its big eyes can see remarkably well, even by the faintest starlight. With half a moon in the sky, the landscape below probably looks to the bat as if it's lit up by a spotlight.

Even without the moon or the stars, this bat could find its way. With its sensitive hearing, it uses **echolocation**, letting out high-pitched sounds and listening to the echoes. Its sense of echolocation is so fine that it can detect objects less than half a millimeter across.

Now the bat swoops down low and begins to hover, staying in one place like a helicopter. A moth, which had paused in its flight to rest on a leafy shrub, did not sense the bat's quick and silent approach. In a moment, it's trapped in the bat's claws.

Quickly the bat finds a perch, pulls the moth apart, and begins to eat it. Soon it will be in the air again, hunting more prey.

Hunters like the California leaf-nosed bat control the insect population of the desert. Without bats eating their prey, there would be too many insects for the ecosystem to bear. Just by catching a meal, these hunters, like other predators, help keep the ecosystem in balance.

Other bats in the Sonoran Desert, like the Mexican long-tongued bat, help the ecosystem in another way. It is a nectar-eating bat, and, like bees and humming-birds, it sucks the nectar from flowers. The flowers of several desert plants, including the saguaro and the agave, are perfectly designed to attract bats. They bloom at

Bats do not only eat the nectar from the plant. While grooming itself, a bat also scrapes extra pollen off its fur and licks it up, adding excellent protein to its diet.

FASCINATING FACT

night, when the bats are active. They are light-colored, easily seen in the dark. And they give off a musty aroma, or a smell like rotting fruit, that isn't particularly attractive to humans but seems like a perfume to bats.

There's a reason that these plants go to so much trouble to attract bats. As the bats eat a flower's nectar, they become dusted with the flower's pollen. When they visit another flower later, some of that pollen will fall off. Once a plant has been **pollinated**, it can do something very important: it can grow seeds. The seeds, with luck, will grow into brand-new plants.

Nectar-eating bats help plants **reproduce**, or make more plants. This is something that every living thing in an ecosystem must try to do. Right now, another creature of the Sonoran Desert ecosystem is attempting it. A male tarantula, about four inches long, covered in bristling hair, crawls out of a one-inch-wide hole in the ground. He is on the lookout for a mate.

Most spiders spin webs out of silk to catch their prey, but the Arizona blond tarantula, like many tarantulas, doesn't. It lives in a burrow that it has dug for itself, and it comes out to hunt, killing animals

Above: A male tarantula.
Opposite: Joshua trees.

The largest spiders in the world are in the tarantula family. The Goliath tarantula of South America has a leg span of twelve inches.

let the female know he's there. Hopefully she'll respond by coming out and letting him mate with her—and hopefully he'll make a successful escape afterward. Sometimes a female tarantula eats the male right after (or even during!) mating. Since the male isn't going to stay around and help her lay eggs or look after the young, once the mating is over, the female sees him mainly as a good source of calories.

Mating is risky for the tarantula, but the chance to have **offspring**, or young, is so important that he's willing to risk it. Unfortunately, however, he's not going to get the chance. A tarantula hawk is winging through the air nearby, and it is a danger to the big spider.

The creature that's threatening the tarantula isn't a bird. It's a large wasp, more

like grasshoppers, beetles, and smaller spiders with its venom. The tarantula's venom wouldn't do serious harm to a person, but it's deadly to the small creatures that become its prey.

The male tarantula that's just crawled out of his burrow, however, has more than food on his mind. He's searching for another burrow, one with a female tarantula inside who's old enough to mate. For a tarantula, this means about ten years old. Most spiders live only a year or two, but tarantulas in the wild can survive up to twenty years.

If the tarantula finds such a burrow, he'll stroke and tap the strands of silk stretched across the entrance, creating vibrations that

If you'd ever had a tarantula hawk sting you, you'd remember it; the sting is considered to be the most painful one that any insect native to the United States or Mexico can deliver.

**FASCINATING FACT**

A tarantula hawk.

than an inch long, with a blue-black body and bright orange wings. The wasp swoops in low, and the tarantula senses danger. He stops moving and goes into a defensive posture, raising his front legs high, ready to attack.

But the wasp takes advantage of the tarantula's pose to dart underneath and sting him near the base of one leg. The tarantula didn't react quickly enough to stop the attacking insect, and now it's too late. The wasp's venom is in his system, and in a very short time the spider goes limp. He can no longer move.

But the tarantula isn't dead, or even dying. He's paralyzed and will remain so for the rest of his life—which isn't going to be pleasant. Now the wasp has some work to do. Working quickly, she digs a burrow in the sandy ground, then drags the tarantula inside. This will be a safe place for her to carry out the next part of her plan.

The wasp wants the tarantula for a meal, but not for herself. She's ready to lay her egg, and once she has dragged the tarantula into the burrow, she does so, leaving the single egg on the spider's back. She makes her way outside the burrow, seals it up, and departs, with the still-living, immobilized tarantula and her egg inside.

When the egg hatches a few days later, the **larva** will find a ready-to-eat meal—the tarantula. It will slowly devour the living, paralyzed spider. This food source will keep the young wasp alive while it changes into its adult form. The next spring a new wasp will emerge from the burrow, leaving behind anything that remains of the tarantula.

The tarantula in search of a mate and the tarantula wasp in search of a meal for her unborn offspring were both on the same mission as the saguaro and the agave when they're blooming with flowers that attract bats. They were trying to reproduce, to make more of their kind. So was the desert tortoise who laid the eggs that the Gila monster found. So was the prickly pear plant, growing tempting, juicy fruit that animals will eat—it was making sure that its seeds get scattered so that new plants could grow. Even the coyote, helping his parents raise his brother and sisters, is trying to accomplish the same thing. He's making sure that young coyotes from his own family survive.

An ecosystem is full of creatures trying to eat and not be eaten, trying to mate or spread their pollen so that they can repro-

Above: Orange cactus blossoms.

Left: A striped whiptail lizard.

Opposite: Sunset over the Sonoran Desert.

duce. As living things struggle to achieve these goals, they all interact in countless complex ways. Sometimes they are predator and prey; sometimes they are pollinator and food. A turtle's eggs feed a Gila monster; a tarantula nourishes a wasp's young; a bat eats nectar and spreads pollen from flower to flower. Each plant and animal in the desert depends on many others. None could survive alone. All these relationships between living things are what make an ecosystem so complex—and so fascinating.

# THE EVERGLADES

Imagine a smooth, shallow river that stretches across the state of Florida. A river that trickles rather than flows, where alligators lurk and panthers hunt, and where brilliant white egrets and sunset pink spoonbills once nested in numbers so great they could not be counted.

That's the Everglades.

Like Monterey Bay, the Everglades is an ecosystem that is all about water. From

**Right: A great white egret glides over the Florida Everglades.**

just south of Orlando, which is about half-way down the long, thin **peninsula** of Florida, water gathers in lakes and streams. Much of that water drains into Lake Okeechobee, farther south. As the water level rises in the lake, it slowly overflows.

Above: A great blue heron in flight.
Below: A Florida treefrog.

The lake water is joined by water from the heavy rains that fall on Florida during its wet season in summer and fall. All that water makes a long, slow journey down to Florida Bay at the southern tip of the state.

The water flows downhill from Lake Okeechobee to the ocean. But since the slope of the land is so gentle and slight, the flow is extremely slow and the water is very shallow. You could wade across most of the Everglades without getting your hair wet. And even if you stood in the water, you wouldn't be able to feel a current.

The flowing water has carved out many different landscapes. There are miles of flat, grassy marshland, where the water trickles through blades of green saw grass. But there are also weedy lakes, shallow meandering rivers called **sloughs**, and humps of dry land called **hammocks**. In some areas there are sandy uplands thick with pine trees. Near the southern tip of Florida, the fresh water meets the salty ocean. Here, mangrove trees grow in the **brackish** (somewhat salty) water, building up islands by trapping mud with their exposed roots. All of these different habitats come together to create the Everglades ecosystem.

A section of this ecosystem is protected by the United States government as the Everglades National Park, which President Harry Truman created in 1947. He called the Everglades a "land, tranquil in its quiet beauty . . . of subtle charm and complexity, preserved forever for the inspiration and enjoyment of mankind." Later, the United Nations made the Everglades into a World Heritage Site, an International Biosphere Reserve, and a Wilderness of International Significance.

An American alligator in the Everglades.

The Everglades provide a home for an amazing variety of plants and animals. There are frogs and toads that fill the air with croaking songs, and herons and egrets that wade with their long, stiltlike legs through the muddy waters. Many types of fish splash and swim through shallow rivers and grassy marshes. Panthers prowl the night and hide in forest dens during the day. And thousands of American alligators bellow, hiss, and hunt in marshy grasslands and shallow rivers.

On a hot day in late summer, one female alligator in the Everglades has been staying close to a pile of plants in a stretch of quiet marsh. Rough-edged blades of saw grass have been heaped up about three feet high, and now a high-pitched croaking noise is coming from the center of this pile of greenery.

About four months ago, the female heard the bellow of a male, called a bull. He made the booming, echoing call by keeping his mouth closed and vibrating the skin of his throat. She could also hear him slapping the water with his head. The two courted each other in alligator fashion, touching snouts, rubbing backs, and

## FASCINATING FACT

Everglades National Park is the third-largest national park in the lower forty-eight states. Only Yellowstone National Park and Death Valley National Park are bigger. The Everglades National Park protects more than 1.5 million acres of land.

swimming in circles around each other. When each was finally convinced that the other was a good choice, they mated. The bull disappeared, and the female cleared a nest site, about seven to ten inches in diameter, in the marsh. She built a mound of mud, leaves, and debris, then dug out a hollow cavity in the dirt. There she laid thirty eggs, covered them up with plants, grass, and weeds, and waited two months.

The green plants in the nest slowly rotted, creating enough heat and energy as they decomposed to keep the eggs warm. This is similar to what happens in a compost pile. The hot Florida sun also did its part to keep the eggs from getting too cold. The mother did not need to sit on her eggs the way birds do, but she did stay nearby, protecting the nest from predators like raccoons, otters, skunks, and gray foxes. All of these animals would be glad to make a meal out of thirty nourishing alligator eggs, and they often do, despite the mother's vigilance.

The heat of the sunlight and the rotting plants didn't just keep the **embryos** alive inside the eggs—they also played a role in determining what sex they would be. If the

eggs stayed at ninety-one degrees Fahrenheit or higher, they would all be male. If they were kept at eighty-five degrees Fahrenheit or lower, they would all be female. Since this particular nest kept the eggs in between those two temperatures, some of the hatchlings will be male, some female. Now,

An alligator hatchling.

about two months after the eggs were laid, the baby alligators are croaking to let their mother know that they are ready to hatch.

The alligator mother clears the plants off the top of the nest. Some of the eggs have cracked open already; others are trembling and rocking. Soon hatchlings are pouring out of the nest and down to the ground. Each is between eight and ten inches long. Clustering around their mother's feet, they let out little hisses and yelps or barks that sound a bit like *Yeonk! Yeonk!*

The babies make sure to stay close to their mother. There are very few things in the Everglades that are a threat to a full-

There are only two species of alligators in the world. One is the American alligator, like those who live in the Everglades. The other is the Chinese alligator, who live in or near the Yangtze River in China.

grown alligator. But the hatchlings are easy, tasty prey for a long list of predators: fish such as bass and gar, big frogs, snakes like water moccasins, snapping turtles, otters, mink, red-shouldered hawks, barred owls, great horned owls, storks, egrets, and cranes. The babies will stay with their mother for about two years, until they have a better chance of survival on their own.

The mother begins to lead her hatchlings away from the nest and through the marsh that surrounds them. Patches of saw grass wave over their heads and stretch out for miles, growing in ground that's covered with an inch or two of muddy water. Then the mother alligator stops. She hears a rustling, dragging sound. Something big is coming, making the saw grass sway. The hatchlings gather around their mother's clawed feet. There is only one thing as big as an alligator in the saw-grass marsh, and that is—another alligator.

The green blades of the saw grass part, and the long, rounded snout of another alligator pokes out. The mother alligator is about seven feet long, an average length for a female. The approaching alligator is bigger, about nine feet—a male. In fact, he might very well be the father of the hatchlings, who are now huddled behind their mother for protection.

The bull alligator is hungry. When he sees the babies, he doesn't recognize the babies as his own. All he sees is a meal.

But the mother alligator has invested a lot of time and energy into making sure

Top: A great horned owl.

Middle: A snapping turtle.

Bottom: An eastern cottonmouth snake, also known as a water moccasin.

that her eggs stayed safe and that her hatchlings survived. She's not about to back off, even in the face of this larger alligator. She lets out a hiss, warning the male

If a bull alligator hears another male bellow, he'll answer by bellowing himself. Sometimes bulls will bellow back at trucks or airplanes going by, mistaking their roaring sounds for the sound of another alligator.

**FASCINATING FACT**

that she'll attack if he doesn't back off.

The bull hesitates, but the female hisses again, louder and longer this time, and he decides that a meal can be gotten more easily. He turns and departs, dragging his long tail behind him, and the mother leads her babies safely on through the tall blades of saw grass.

Dense stands of saw grass like the one the alligators are walking through wave and ripple across many square miles of the Everglades. This tough, grasslike plant can grow up to twelve feet high, and it has sharp edges, **serrated** like a saw, which is where it gets its name.

Like most of the Everglades, the saw-grass marsh is a wetland. This means just what it sounds like—land that's often wet or flooded. Summer and fall are the wet season in the Everglades, and rainfall floods rivers, ponds, and marshes. The rainfall helps turn the saw-grass marsh into an important source of food for many of the animals who live there.

Above: An American alligator floats among the plantlife in the waters of the Everglades.

Opposite: A section of saw-grass marsh.

Riverine grass shrimp are nearly transparent. This makes it hard for predators to spot them in the water.

**FASCINATING FACT**

There are very few animals that eat saw grass. But when the saw-grass marsh is flooded, as it is now, algae grows on the stems of the grass. It grows on anything else underwater, too—other plants, washed-up sticks, animal bones, even the mud. This algae is the base for most of the food chains in the Everglades.

Right now, small fish are nibbling the algae that grows on the saw grass as the alligator and her hatchlings splash through the shallow waters of the marsh. Tiny least killifish, each only a few centimeters long, and flagfish, with stripes of red and silvery white, are feasting. A tadpole lingers too

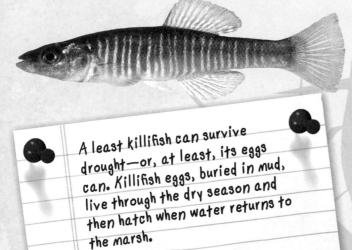

A least killifish can survive drought—or, at least, its eggs can. Killifish eggs, buried in mud, live through the dry season and then hatch when water returns to the marsh.

Opposite: A great white heron hunts in the shallow water of the Everglades.

long at her meal, and one of the alligator hatchlings snatches the tiny amphibian up in his jaws. These little water creatures are too small for the mother alligator to be interested in, but they're perfect for the hatchlings. As the baby alligators grow, they'll move on to frogs, bigger fish, and insects, like dragonflies.

Riverine grass shrimp (also called freshwater prawns) are eating the algae, too. Dark brown apple snails, which can grow to two inches across as adults, cling to the stems of the saw grass. They crawl underwater down the stems to eat the algae and crawl back up into the air to breathe.

As the alligator and her hatchlings move through the marsh, another predator swoops low overhead. The snail kite is a hunting bird, about the size of a small hawk. It glimpses the hungry fish eating the algae, and a crayfish scuttling along the mud among the grasses, but it's not interested in these things. The snail kite eats only one thing—apple snails. The kite swoops down and hovers over the water to

An Everglades kite.

Apple snail

than a foot long, has been drifting motion-less near the surface. It looks like a stick floating in the water, and maybe that's what the bluegill thinks it is. When the smaller fish is close enough, the gar flicks its fins to bring it alongside. Then, with a sideways snap of its long, skinny snout, it has the bluegill trapped in it needle-sharp teeth.

The gar, the bluegill, the apple snail, the kite, and many other creatures of the Everglades depend on the algae in the marsh or upon the creatures who eat the

snatch a snail in its talons, and transfers the snail to its beak as it flies. Finding a perch a little way off, it uses its curved beak to pluck the snail from its shell.

Other predators are also interested in the small creatures who graze on the algae of the saw-grass marsh. A bluegill snaps up a least killifish, and then darts toward slightly deeper water. This turns out to be a mistake for the bluegill. It didn't notice a bigger fish lying in wait—a Florida gar.

The gar, a thin, dark brown fish more

Bluegill

algae for their food. And the algae depends on something else—water. Algae needs water to grow. During the wet season, the fish and small **invertebrates** who eat the algae thrive, and so do the predators who hunt them. But winter and spring are dry seasons in the Everglades. Little rain falls. Rivers get shallower; ponds shrink; marshes dry up. The lack of water can be a problem for many wetland animals. Luckily, the alligators who live in the marsh provide a solution—they dig alligator holes.

The alligator whose babies have just hatched is leading her young through the saw-grass marsh toward her own alligator hole. Several years ago, the mother alligator found a shallow pool in the marsh. As the dry season began and the marsh started to dry up, this pool still held a little bit of

The Florida gar has very hard, sharp scales. Native Americans once used the scales to make arrowheads.

An American alligator.

Above: An anhinga perched on a fallen log.
Opposite: A soft-shelled turtle.

The anhinga has been called the snakebird. When it swims with only its head and neck out of water, it can look a little like a snake.

**FASCINATING FACT**

water. The alligator returned there to hunt. While trying to find food that was hidden in the muck at the bottom of the pool, or trying to herd fish toward the bank where she could catch them more easily, she plowed up the mud with her tail and shoveled it away with her face and head. As a result, the pool became deeper, creating what's known as an alligator hole.

Each year, as the dry season began, the alligator returned to the pool. Each year she dug it deeper. Now it's about twenty feet across, and perhaps three feet deep. Water from the marsh drains into it, keeping it full even in the dry season. Now the alligator (and her offspring) always have a place to find water, swim, and hunt. The mother alligator is only willing to share the hole with her young. And while other animals use the hole, for the most part other alligators stay away.

The alligator hole is important not only for the alligator family. Many other animals depend on it, too. The arrival of the mother and the hatchlings disturbs some of them. As the mother pushes through the saw grass and past a fringe of cattails and the purple flowers of alligator flag to reach the hole, a soft-shelled turtle slides from the bank into the water. A muskrat darts into a hole. A pig frog's croaking, sounding like the grunting of a farmyard pig, is suddenly hushed. A large bird called an anhinga glides through the water with only its neck and head visible and then hops out onto a half-sunken log, holding its wings out. Unlike most water birds, the anhinga has no oil on its feathers to keep them waterproof. Wet feathers make the bird cold, so it holds its wings open to let the sun reach its body and warm it up.

The alligator slips into the water while her hatchlings wait on the bank. She holds her legs tight against her sides and wiggles her body to swim. Then she coasts to a

A soft-shelled turtle can "snorkel," swimming completely underwater while breathing with its long nose extended above the water's surface.

stop, with only her nostrils showing above the murky water. If you didn't know better, you might think she was nothing but a floating log.

Suddenly the alligator lunges forward. Her jaws, with their eighty teeth, clamp around the prey she's spotted—a soft-shelled turtle. The turtle that slid into the water earlier from the bank did not get far enough away, and now the alligator has it in her jaws, which can press downward with a force of three thousand pounds per square inch.

But even so, the turtle's shell doesn't crack. A soft-shelled turtle's shell is covered with skin and is soft at the edges; that's where the turtle gets its name. But that doesn't mean the shell is weak. It's still strong enough to protect the turtle from most things—maybe even from the jaws of a hungry alligator. The turtle pulls its legs and head inside, trying to do the only thing it can—wait for a chance to escape.

The alligator isn't giving up easily, however. She returns to the bank with the turtle in her mouth. Her hatchlings watch as she tosses the turtle into the air and catches it before it falls, biting down hard. She does this again and again. Finally the shell gives in. It cracks and the alligator crunches up the turtle, swallowing bones, shell, and all.

Alligators don't prey only on turtles. They will eat nearly anything they come across. They'll snap up swimming prey—fish, turtles, frogs, ducks. Or they will wait quietly, mostly underwater, for an animal like a raccoon or a deer to come to the water's edge to drink. The prey may be quickly grabbed in those strong jaws and swallowed whole, or, if it's larger, pulled into the water and drowned.

It's dangerous for these animals to come near an alligator hole. But in the dry season, they have no choice. As the marsh dries up around them, water-dwelling creatures like fish, snails, crabs, shrimp, frogs, and crayfish are trapped in alligator holes. They become food for predators like the

Top: A gray fox.
Middle: A muskrat eating a cattail root.
Bottom: A raccoon.

A great white heron hunting for prey.

muskrat and anhinga and the soft-shelled turtle. Snakes come to feed. At night, gray foxes, raccoons, and opossums arrive to get a drink and see what kind of meal they can find. All of these animals, predator and prey alike, depend on the alligator hole for survival until the rains come again to flood the marsh.

By digging her hole, the alligator makes sure she will always have water and prey to eat. But her prey benefits others, too; the alligator hole creates a place for animals to live and to hunt. The alligator is helping the very species she depends on for food. She needs them; they need her. Like the wolves and elk in Yellowstone, like otters in Monterey Bay and the urchins they

prey on, like bats and the Sonoran Desert flowers they pollinate, each part of the ecosystem needs the other.

As the alligator settles down on the bank of her hole to rest in the sun, and as some of her hatchlings crawl fearlessly onto her head and back to **bask**, a snowy egret, named for its snow-white feathers, flaps over to the pool and begins to fish. It doesn't seem worried about the resting alligator as it wades slowly through the water, using its big, bright yellow feet to stir up the mud. When an inch-long mosquitofish darts away from those feet, the egret's sharp bill is ready to snap it up.

Wading birds like the egret are among the many animals who depend on the prey

that gather at alligator holes, and who in turn sometimes provide prey for alligators. There are fourteen kinds of large wading birds in the Everglades. All of them (like the egret) have long legs that make it easy for them to wade through the shallow water and long beaks that are good for stabbing or scooping up fish, crayfish, tadpoles, and insect eggs or larvae to eat.

Some wading birds of the Everglades—such as roseate spoonbills with their pink feathers and oddly shaped bills, tricolor herons, and especially white ibis—gather together in groups called rookeries to build nests, lay eggs, and raise hatchlings. One rookery can have as many as thousands of birds.

Once the eggs hatch and the hatchlings have grown old enough to look after themselves, the birds fly away. Some stay in the Everglades; some scatter beyond Florida, either north or south to the tropics. Most

Above: A glossy ibis wading among some weeds.
Opposite: Roseate spoonbills.

Big wading birds like herons and ibises were nearly wiped out of the Everglades by a surprising enemy—ladies' fashion. In the late 1800s, nearly every woman in America wore a hat with feathers on it. Women especially loved long, white egret feathers. Special egret plumes, which the birds grow only in their mating season, sold for thirty-two dollars an ounce during the 1800s. At the end of the nineteenth century, an ounce of egret plumes cost twice as much as an ounce of gold.

With so much money to be made from birds' feathers, hunters invaded the Everglades, often tracking birds to their rookeries. They would kill the adults, take the feathers, and leave the bodies to rot or be eaten by scavengers. The eggs in the nest would be smashed or simply left unhatched. After many years, laws were finally passed to protect the birds, but it was easy to break the law in this remote area. The only thing that saved the birds was a change in fashion. Suddenly women were not as interested in wearing feathered hats anymore, and the numbers of wading birds in the Everglades began to increase again.

will return to the Everglades when they are ready to breed, forming new rookeries of their own.

Wading birds find safe nesting sites and abundant prey in the Everglades. As they prey on fish and other water-dwelling creatures, they help keep the populations of these animals in balance. And the birds also provide food for predators like alligators who hunt in the marshes and rivers. Like all the living things within an ecosystem, they are part of a complicated web of life and death, with each strand connected to others.

The snowy egret, hunting at the alligator hole, is participating in that complicated web of survival. Her presence may mean death for some of the fish around her feet. Or it may mean her own death if she doesn't stay far enough away from the mother alligator resting on the bank. At the moment, the alligator seems more interested in soaking up the heat of the sun, so, snatching up a crayfish and gulping it down, the egret continues hunting. She doesn't notice a set of footprints in the muddy bank as she passes by them.

Each print, about two inches wide, shows the mark of one large pad, a triangular shape with rounded corners. There are also four ovals where toes pressed into the

Panther tracks.

mud. There are no marks of claws, which is a clue about the animal that left this print. It can't have been a fox or a black bear or a raccoon; those animals would all leave claw marks. This set of footprints was left by a Florida panther. Like all cats, the panther's claws can retract, or slide back inside its paws, when it's walking or resting.

A female panther came down to the alligator hole last night. Panthers normally prefer the slightly higher areas of the Everglades, the sandy uplands or the hammocks that lie above flood level. But they

A Florida panther.

Panthers are also called pumas, painters, catamounts, cougars, mountain lions, and swamp screamers.

sometimes come down into the marshy areas in the dark to hunt.

There are more than twenty **subspecies** of panthers living in North and South America, in every habitat from snow-covered mountain to desert to rain forest to swamp. Florida panthers once roamed the southern part of the United States, from Arkansas to South Carolina to Florida, but only a small population—about fifty to seventy panthers—still claim the Everglades as their home. Many have a tail with a kink, or twist, on the end, and a ridge of hair along the back, setting them apart from other panther subspecies. They are also the smallest of all panthers. Since they live in a warm climate, they don't need the layer of fat under the skin that other panthers have to protect them from the cold.

Most people will never see a Florida panther. These cats hunt mainly at night or twilight. Even if they are active during the day, they are very hard to spot. With their smooth, tawny coats and their skill at stay-ing perfectly immobile, they blend in with the trees and brush.

Tonight, after darkness falls, the panther returns to the alligator hole. She slinks into the saw grass, settling down in a crouch and waiting. Like most cats, she can see well in very dim light, although not in complete darkness. But the moon hanging in the sky gives her enough light for a clear view of the alligator hole and any animals who might arrive there. Panthers depend more on sight and on their keen hearing than on smell to track down prey.

After a while, an opossum comes along a trampled path in the saw grass. This small, gray mammal, with her long, pointed nose, small eyes, and bare tail, is ready for a drink. She can't smell the panther so near her. A light breeze rattles the saw grass and blows the panther's scent away from the opossum.

When the opossum gets to the pool's edge and settles down to drink, the panther creeps out of the saw grass, inching

An opossum's front paw print normally measures 1 3/4" and the back is 2" in length.

back          front

A young opossum.

closer. Like most cats, she can make a quick dash, but she can't run fast for a long period of time. She'll have the best chance of making this catch if she can get close to the opossum without it seeing her.

Slowly, paw by paw, belly close to the ground, the cat creeps nearer and nearer. The opossum lifts its head from the water, its nose twitching, checking the breeze. Then, as it turns to go, it catches sight of the big, pale brown predator in the moonlight. The opossum tries to scuttle to safety—but the panther is already moving. Her powerful back legs push her forward in a tremendous leap, and she lands with her front paws squarely on top of the opossum. One quick bite to the back of the neck, and the opossum is dead in the panther's claws.

It all happens so quickly that the opossum didn't even have a chance to try its emergency tactic of playing dead. If startled, an opossum will often flop to the ground and lie without moving. Many predators are interested only in prey that

Opossum playing dead.

mother on her nightly hunting trips. She made sure they were safely hidden before she went to the alligator hole to hunt the opossum. Now she brings them back, and they all begin to feed. The mother gets most of the opossum's meat; she's bigger and needs more to keep up her strength. But the kittens each get a few scraps, which they devour hungrily. If the mother panther had killed a larger animal—a deer, maybe—she would bury whatever she and her kittens couldn't eat, coming back to finish it later. But the opossum is small enough that pretty soon only her bones are left.

Then their mother leads the kittens back through the saw-grass marsh. They keep going, heading for the higher ground and their den, when they come across something strange.

The cats feel a flat, hard surface underfoot—a highway. Cautiously, the panther family ventures out onto this unfamiliar surface. And then they hear a sound in the distance, the growl of a car, coming quickly

moves; they might leave the opossum alone if she looks like she's already dead. But we'll never know if this trick would have succeeded with the panther.

The panther does not settle down to eat her kill. Instead, she moves off into the saw grass. But in a minute or two she is back, with two kittens trotting behind her.

The panther kittens have spotted coats, which help to keep them hidden in their den in the heart of a thicket of palmetto, a type of low-growing palm tree. The spots blend in among the dappled splashes of light and shadow under the palmetto fronds. They were born three or four months ago, tiny, small, and blind. Each weighed close to one pound. They did little but sleep and drink their mother's milk. After about two or three weeks, their eyes opened and they grew strong enough to play and wrestle and wander about their den. While their mother went out hunting, the two kittens chased each other, pounced on palmetto fronds, and chewed bits of sticks, exercising and getting stronger as they waited for the big panther to return.

When they were about two months old, the panther kittens began to go with their

Panther kittens are born with bright blue eyes. Their eyes will change to brown as they grow.

**FASCINATING FACT**

continue on their way. Soon they are climbing a slight hill, and the ground under their feet becomes less muddy and more sandy. They've reached a hammock, a hill that rises a little bit above the level of the marsh.

Hammocks are not wetlands; they are high enough to escape the regular flooding that sweeps through the Everglades marshes every wet season. Plants that could not live in the marsh can grow here, such as live oak with its small leaves and low, spreading branches; short, stubby cabbage palms; and strangler figs. And many animals find a home here, too.

A raccoon stays safely up a tree until the panther and her kittens have gone by. A

A panther crossing sign warns drivers passing through the Florida Everglades.

and steadily nearer. The mother panther leaps backward into some bushes, and one of the kittens hurries after her. But the other seems confused.

The car gets closer, and the kitten crouches down on the road and hisses, as if he could scare the car away. Then he leaps up and races to his mother's side just as the car rushes past, its wheel only a few inches from the kitten's tail. Cars are a huge danger to the population of Florida panthers. Since panthers are active mostly at night, it's hard for drivers to see them.

The cats wait by the highway awhile, as if making sure that no more cars will come. Then they dash across the road and

A strangler fig often sprouts from a seed that's landed in the top of another tree. It then sends roots down to the ground. Eventually the roots completely surround the other tree, which is slowly killed by the shade of the strangler fig.

A Florida panther.

large barred owl flits overhead. A few minutes later, its unique call drifts through the shadowy night forest. Some people think it sounds as if the owl is calling, "Who cooks for you? Who cooks for you all?" In the daylight, a visitor to the hammock might spot a tree snail clinging to the bark of a tree, a red or yellow Everglades rat snake coiled high in a tree, or a small black lizard with a neon blue tail—a blue-tailed skink—skittering along the forest floor.

Like many of the animals around them, the panther and her kittens could not survive in the Everglades if they had nowhere to live but the often-flooded saw-grass marsh. But the dry hilltop that is the hammock provides them with a good home. As they make their way through the forest, the

If an Everglades rat snake feels threatened, it might coil its body and rustle its tail in dry leaves so that it sounds like a rattlesnake. It can also climb trees or swim to escape danger.

mother stops to sniff at a fallen gumbo-limbo tree. Humans have used the sap of this tall tree with glossy, bright green leaves for making glue and varnish, but the panther will use it for something else—to mark her territory. She rubs her face against the log, just the way you might see a pet cat rub up against a table or chair. She's leaving a scent on the log that other panthers will be able to detect. Then she unsheathes her claws and uses them to mark the papery bark with long scratches. These are signs to show that no other panther is welcome in this particular part of the hammock. If another panther sees the scratches on the tree and smells the markings left by the mother panther, it will know to keep away. Each panther has its own territory, and will defend it by fighting if it has to.

Along with cars, fights between panthers in the Everglades are a major cause of death for the big cats. Each male panther needs about two hundred square miles to himself; each female needs around seventy square miles. When there is not much living space for big, **territorial** predators like panthers, they meet each other more often than they ordinarily would. Fights are common, and may lead to one panther being killed, or to one or both being so badly wounded that they can't hunt. Big predators need lots of space if they are to go about their normal lives in safety.

A barred owl.

Panthers need space to roam and hunt. Alligators need room to lay their eggs. White ibis and snail kites and hundreds of other birds need safe places for their nests. And every living thing in the Everglades needs the water that falls from the sky and trickles slowly, inch by inch, from Lake Okeechobee to the ocean.

Just as in Yellowstone, the Everglades

National Park, where land, plants, and animals are protected, is only part of a larger ecosystem. And outside the national park preserved area, the land and water that make up the Everglades ecosystem has been changing for years. Today about half of the ecosystem has been planted with farms or made into towns. People have dammed rivers and drained marshes and built roads or houses and planted fields of sugarcane. All of this has interfered with the natural flow of water that makes the Everglades ecosystem what it is.

Once the water flowed naturally from Lake Okeechobee to Florida Bay, pulled slowly south by nothing more than gravity. Now there are sixteen hundred miles of canals, **levees**, and **spillways** in the Everglades, all meant to control how the water moves. But changing one part of the ecosystem—in this case, the water—means changes to the rest. As people interfered with the flow of water in the Everglades, the flocks of herons, egrets, and ibis grew smaller. They no longer nest in the Everglades in numbers too big to be counted. Florida panthers are so endangered they may not survive at all.

But people are beginning to make some changes that will help bring the ecosystem

of the Everglades back. In 2000, the United States government and the state of Florida agreed to begin work on restoring the Everglades. They planned to spend billions of dollars and thirty years, working on eighteen thousand square miles, trying to bring back the flow of water closer to what it once was. It is the largest project ever

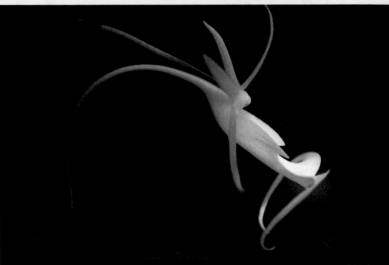

Above: A ghost orchid; one of a wide variety of orchids that grow in the lush Everglades.

Below: A blue-tailed skink.

Opposite: Black-necked stilts.

undertaken to restore a wilderness area.

In 2008, the restoration of the Everglades made a big step forward. A company called U.S. Sugar agreed to sell the land it owned in the Everglades to the government. By 2014, it will no longer plant sugarcane on the fields just south of Lake

Above: A Florida river otter taking a drink of water.
Below: A blue dragonfly on a blade of grass.
Opposite: Pink flamingos.

Okeechobee. Instead, the land will be protected. One hundred and eighty thousand acres will become marshland and **reservoirs** to hold water that will be allowed once more to flow naturally through the Everglades.

The plan to restore the Everglades is complicated. It will need a lot of work. But this amazing place might return to an ecosystem where alligators bellow, ibis gather in flocks too big to be counted, panthers hiss and howl in the night, and saw grass waves over mile and mile of peaceful marsh and shallow rivers.

Each piece of this delicate ecosystem depends on every other piece. Think of the rain that falls and fills lakes and rivers and marshes, the algae who live in the water the rains bring, the fish who eat the algae and the birds who eat the fish, and the alligator who digs holes where fish can live and birds and opossums and panthers can come to drink and hunt. Every one of these animals and plants, every drop of rain, affects the ecosystem in some way. Only if all these parts work together as they should can the Everglades continue to be a complicated, beautiful ecosystem where so many kinds of life can thrive.

# GLOSSARY

**bask:** to rest in sunlight, usually in order to warm up

**bioluminescence:** light that is produced by living organisms

**blade:** the flat part of a leaf

**brackish:** slightly salty; a mixture of salty and fresh water

**burrow:** a hole made by an animal for shelter

**caldera:** a volcanic crater

**cold seep:** a source of life in the deep ocean; liquid rich in sulfide seeps out of cracks in the sea floor

**crustacean:** an animal, such as a lobster, shrimp, or crab, with a hard shell and many jointed legs

**dorsal:** on the back

**echolocation:** the ability to locate objects by emitting sounds and listening to the echoes

**embryo:** an animal that hasn't yet been born or hatched

**estivate:** to spend time in a dormant state, with very little activity, during the summer or during a drought

**food chain:** the relationship between living things, each of which feeds on another. A simple food chain would be grass—elk—wolves.

**geothermic:** relating to the heat in the center of the earth

**geyser:** a spring that releases jets of heated water and steam

**gills:** organs in fish that take in oxygen from water

**gland:** an organ in the body that either secretes (puts out) or absorbs a certain substance from the bloodstream

**habitat:** the space and natural conditions (like temperature or weather) in which a particular species can survive. Many habitats can be contained inside an ecosystem.

**hammock:** a fertile area higher than its surroundings

**herbivore:** an animal that eats plants.

**invertebrate:** an animal without a backbone

**kelpshed:** pieces of kelp torn off by waves and currents

**larva:** the young form of an animal, often an insect. The larval form is different in shape from the adult form. A caterpillar is a larval form of a butterfly. *Larvae* is the plural of *larva*.

**levee:** an embankment, or small ridge or hill, built along a river to hold back its waters

**magma:** molten, or melted, rock under the surface of the earth

**mucus:** a clear, slimy substance produced by the body

**nocturnal:** active at night

**offspring:** children, young

**peninsula:** a long, thin arm of land, surrounded by water on three sides but attached to land on the fourth side

**photosynthesis:** the process by which a plant absorbs energy from the sun and uses it to produce food for itself

**pollinate:** to transfer pollen, or spores, from one plant to another

**reproduce:** to have offspring, or young. For an animal, this usually means mating and laying eggs or giving birth to babies. For a plant, it usually means growing seeds that can grow into more plants.

**reservoir:** a place where water is collected for use in the future

**rodent:** an animal, such as a mouse, squirrel, or beaver, that has large front teeth for gnawing

**rumen:** the large first compartment of the stomach of a ruminant, like a cow

**ruminants:** plant-eating animals, such as sheep, cattle, and deer, that chew their cud (chew again plants that have been swallowed)

**serrated:** resembling a sharp-toothed edge of a saw

**slough:** an inlet or a river

**spawn:** offspring; to produce offspring

**spillway:** a channel for carrying away extra water

**stipe:** a stemlike structure that connects the holdfast and blade of algae, like kelp

**subspecies:** a group of animals within a species that have particular traits, like the kinked tail and ridge of back fur on a Florida panther

**territorial:** an animal that keeps to a certain area, and that will fight to protect that area from other members of its own species

**vertebrate:** an animal with a backbone

**whalefall:** a single whale carcass that has sunk to the ocean floor